# SCANDALOUS
## NEWPORT
# RHODE ISLAND

# SCANDALOUS
## NEWPORT
# RHODE ISLAND

LARRY STANFORD

THE
History
PRESS

Published by The History Press
Charleston, SC 29403
www.historypress.net

First published 2013

ISBN 978-1-5402-2162-9

Library of Congress CIP data applied for.

# CONTENTS

# PREFACE

*Scandalous Newport, Rhode Island* is a result of the popularity of the first incarnation of this idea, *Wicked Newport*, detailing some of Newport's most scintillating scandals, eccentric characters and unsolved mysteries. After receiving numerous suggestions and ideas from readers and fans of the first book, there appeared to be sufficient stories to weave into a second publication.

*Scandalous Newport* is a collaboration of input from Newport locals, as well as personal research to uncover some even more outrageous and previously underexplored narratives while keeping the subject matter as relevant to Newport as possible.

Newport, Rhode Island, is a wonderful place in terms of both historical occurrences and natural beauty. The multiple layers of history and the perpetual reinvention of the city and its image are some of the things that make Newport so unique. It is a place that has been enjoyed by numerous generations and hopefully countless more to come. It is my hope that within these chapters, a small piece of this charming town's history will be preserved. It was really my intention to convey, through these small snapshots of the past, the diverse and distinctive events that have occurred here, as well as to introduce you to some unique people who have graced Newport with their presence.

I hope you enjoy *Scandalous Newport* and any time you have to spend in the "City by the Sea." It is truly a one-of-a-kind place.

# CHAPTER 1

# SHE COULDN'T STAY AWAY

Did Newport, Rhode Island, suffer through a similar mania like the one that transpired during the witch trials of its northern neighbor, Salem, Massachusetts, in the 1690s? Did Newport hold court proceedings for people who espoused the teachings of Satan? Were Newport citizens accused of blasphemy and put to death in front of the entire town? Did superstitions and rumors create a frenzy in which people were terrified that the devil himself walked amongst them? Well, the short answer is no. Newport, upon its founding in 1639, was a haven for all religions. This freedom was eventually guaranteed by a colonial charter from King Charles II in 1663 and deemed a "lively experiment" to allow a person to practice any religion of his or her choosing. Unfortunately, the same could not be said of Boston, which expelled and even executed dissenters who did not completely follow the doctrines of the Puritan faith.

However, Newport did have one citizen who constantly preached her beliefs to the point where she was expelled from Boston, told never to return by the Puritan powers to be and threatened to be put to death if she ever set foot in Boston again. Yet despite all these warnings, she constantly returned, over and over again, to the very place where she could be executed for her religious beliefs. Finally, one day, the threats of capital punishment became reality, and she was hanged in Boston Common for her beliefs about God, religion and faith. Her name was Mary (Barrett) Dyer.

Mary Barrett was born in England around 1611 and married William Dyer in London in 1633. Records indicate that the couple immigrated to the Massachusetts Bay Colony around 1635. Soon after the couple's arrival, problems would arise for Mary Dyer. Originally a puritan herself, Mary was intrigued by the teachings of a local Quaker named Anne Hutchinson, who promoted the radical idea that God could actually speak directly to his followers and not just through the clergy. Of course, this flew in the face of everything the Puritan clergy preached at that time. God spoke only through them! Eventually, Anne Hutchinson was tried and convicted of heresy and exiled from the Massachusetts Bay Colony. Anne Hutchinson and her followers were labeled "Antinomians," after the idea that members of a particular religious group are under no obligation to obey the laws of ethics or morality as presented by religious authorities. So Anne Hutchinson and her small band of godless souls did what everyone else who was banned from Boston did: they moved to Rhode Island. The Antinomians finally settled at the northern tip of Aquidneck Island in a town they named Pocasset. (The town is Portsmouth, Rhode Island, today.) Mary's husband, William, was on of the eighteen men who signed the town's compact. All should have been well for this little band of religious seekers, but more bad news was on the way.

It seems that Massachusetts Bay Colony governor John Winthrop would do everything in his power to discredit any new religious movement that could threaten his position as a religious zealot. Winthrop had discovered that while living in Boston, Mary Dyer had given birth to a stillborn baby that was hastily buried before the Antinomian exile from Boston. Winthrop ordered that the fetus be exhumed and an autopsy performed on the remains. What was uncovered was truly shocking.

Governor Winthrop was obsessed with the fetus, studying the twisted remains endlessly. The mangled fetus was horribly deformed and, in his words,

> *of ordinary bigness: it had a face, but no head, and the ears stood upon the shoulders and were like an ape's; it had no forehead but over the eyes were four horns, hard and sharp. Between the shoulders, it had 2 mouths and in each of them a piece of red flesh sticking out; it had arms and legs as other children do but, instead of toes, it had on each foot three claws, like a young fowl, with sharp talons.*

Whatever your religious beliefs were at this time, this creature, human or otherworldly, was a hideous sight to behold. Winthrop was certain of the mangled fetus's origin. It was a devil child, sent as punishment by God, and was hard and fast evidence of the heresy and sacrilege of the Antinomians.

Up to this point, Mary Dyer was just a devotee of Anne Hutchinson and her wild beliefs. In 1652, however, this would officially change. Mary and her husband would travel back to England with Providence founder Roger Williams and an early leader of the Baptist faith, John Clark. It was on this visit that Mary's life would be forever altered. After hearing the preaching of Society of Friends founder George Fox, Mary Dyer was hooked. She immediately became a Quaker. While William returned to Pocasset later in 1652, Mary remained in England to strengthen her beliefs and become a Quaker preacher herself.

Mary finally returned to the colonies in 1657 and arrived in—where else?—Boston, where she was immediately arrested. She had sailed there to protest a new law that banned Quakers from the strictly Puritan city. Her protests were rejected, of course, and she was once again banished from the Massachusetts Bay Colony and told that if she returned, she would be executed.

But Mary Dyer would not be intimidated by the Puritans and continued to preach her newfound faith throughout all of New England and even into New York. She was not received warmly in most places, as is evident by her arrest and expulsion from New Haven, Connecticut, in 1658. Later that year, the determined Mary Dyer heard of an arrest of two Quaker ministers in Boston, so despite the threat of execution if she were detected, she returned to the Forbidden City to plead for their release. Mary once again was arrested, threatened with hanging and sent on her way. By this time, William had moved south on Aquidneck Island and was living on an eighty-seven-acre farm just north of the burgeoning harbor area of Newport. As you might recall, Newport was a town founded on the principles of religious freedom. Mary Dyer was safe to live here and espouse any doctrine she wished without fear of capital punishment. Yet there was something inside this woman that would not allow her to sit still. She could not rest until all citizens of New England shared the same freedom as she did. The fire of devotion burned so hot inside Mary Dyer that she once again returned to Boston to protest the trial of two condemned Quakers.

This time, the Puritan elders had seen enough of this religious troublemaker. Mary Dyer was sentenced to hang along with the other two condemned Quakers she had traveled to assist. After watching her compatriots die on a rope hanging from a tree in Boston Common in front of a huge gathered audience, it was Mary Dyer's turn to depart this life. She was blindfolded; her hands and feet were bound, and she was led up a ladder with the noose placed around her neck. Just as the ladder was about to be kicked out from under the condemned soul, a voice cried out from the crowd, "Halt the execution!" The new governor, John Endicott, himself stopped the hanging as a personal favor to Mary's husband. However, Mary was warned that this was her last reprieve. If she set foot again in Boston, she would hang.

Mary and William returned to Newport and went back to their daily routines. But once again, the fire of devotion burned so hot inside her that this relentless woman would once again tempt fate and return to the Forbidden City in May 1660. What would drive someone who had a life of safety and comfort in Newport to endlessly return to a place of grave

This statue of Quaker martyr Mary Dyer stands in front of the Massachusetts State Capital, directly across the street from where she was hanged and buried in an unmarked grave. She repeatedly returned to Boston to stand up for what she believed in and eventually paid the ultimate price. *Photo courtesy of the author.*

danger? Was it an obsession or a devotion to a new religion, or was Mary Dyer brainwashed by the teachings of the Quaker faith?

Whatever the reason, she returned to Boston again and was, of course, arrested and sentenced to death. Despite pleas from her husband and family, Mary Dyer was ready to die for her beliefs. She was even offered a last-minute reprieve by Governor Endicott. All she had to do was disavow her Quaker beliefs. But the middle-aged mother of six would not repent, and the Puritans finally executed this "religious menace" on Boston Common in front of a large crowd on June 1, 1660. Mary's last words were: "Nay, I cannot, for in obedience to the will of the Lord, I came. And in his will I abide, faithful to the death."

With those final words, Mary Dyer was put to death for the crime of being a Quaker in Boston.

One Puritan witness had an interesting observation about the hanging. He remarked, "She did hang as a flag, for others to take notice by."

Mary's lifeless body was quickly cut down from the gallows and hastily buried in a shallow, unmarked grave in Boston Common. The exact spot is still unknown to this day. When news of the execution reached England, King Charles II was outraged and banned all further executions of Quakers in Boston. But the damage had already been done; Mary Dyer was dead.

What did her execution really accomplish? The Puritans were a group of repressive and insecure religious zealots who controlled their congregations through fear and superstition. The tide of religious tolerance was changing in the New World. Many colonists were moving away from the hard-line Puritans to the more tolerant Baptist and Quaker faiths. So perhaps Mary Dyer did not die in vain after all. Perhaps her continued efforts to gain freedom of choice in religion paved the way for our freedom to worship as we wish today. King Charles II did grant Rhode Island a charter that promised citizens freedom to worship in 1663, perhaps as a gesture of sorrow in the wake of the Dyer hanging. So next time you sit down in the church of your choice and worship the God you do, say a small prayer of thanks to all the religious pioneers like Mary Dyer who made your freedom of religion a reality.

## CHAPTER 2

# MURDER AT THE WHITE HORSE TAVERN

Just about every colonial town that predates the American Revolution makes the claim of possessing the oldest tavern in the United States. Newport, Rhode Island, is no exception. The White Horse Tavern might actually have the goods to back up its claim. Francis Brinley erected part of the original structure in 1652 and sold the property to a man named William Mayes Sr. in 1673. The property was then enlarged to its present dimensions and has presided over the corner of Marlborough and Farewell Streets ever since. In 1687, a tavern license was obtained, and upon William's passing, his son William Mayes Jr. took over the reins. William Jr. had an interesting side job; besides being a tavern owner, he was also a privateer. A privateer was a legal pirate who held an official charter from the colonial governor and had the legal authority to plunder commercial shipping, seize the shipments and sell off the cargoes, including slaves, at a profit. The charter also stipulated that half of the profits obtained would be delivered to the governor who granted the charter. Needless to say, privateering was a lucrative endeavor for all parties involved, except of course those who had their ships and cargoes seized.

So besides having a notorious owner, the White Horse Tavern also had an illustrious career as a courthouse for the infamous Thomas Cornell trial and as the meeting place for the colonial legislature. It is currently a fine dining restaurant. During the building's lifetime, it also served as a boardinghouse for visiting eighteenth-century sailors who had arrived at Newport's busting harbor. It is because of the actions of one of these eighteenth-century seafarers that the White Horse Tavern acquired its infamous and ghostly reputation, which continues to this day. Its status as one of the most haunted buildings in all of Newport, as you will soon see, is well deserved.

One evening in the early 1720s, two men arrived off a ship that had sailed into Newport Harbor. John and Mary Nichols were now the owners of the tavern and offered the men food and a place to sleep for the evening. In those days, travelers slept where they could, sometimes in barns, on unrolled mattresses or even on blankets on the floor near fireplaces. These two unknown seamen slept on the second floor on thin mattresses unfurled next to the large fireplace. The night passed without incident, and Mary Nichols and her Native American assistant awoke early the next morning to prepare breakfast for the overnight guests. Something was amiss, however. The visitors never came downstairs for breakfast.

When Mary and her assistant went up the narrow staircase to investigate, they were shocked at what they found. One of the unknown guests lay dead where he slept, right next to the large stone fireplace, and the second man was gone. There was no sign of a struggle, no visible wounds, not a drop of blood, but the dead man's belongings were missing along with the second mystery visitor, vanishing overnight into thin air. In those days, smallpox was a huge concern, and since Mary and the native girl had come in contact with a dead body, the two ladies were rushed off to quarantine on Coaster's Island, the current site of the Naval War College. The deceased victim was quickly buried in Newport's Common Burying Ground to prevent the spread of any infectious disease he might have carried. Unfortunately, the worst fears came to pass; both Mary and the Native American housekeeper contracted smallpox from their nameless victim. Fortunately, Mary would survive the ordeal, but the native girl was not so lucky. She succumbed to the disease a short time later.

What actually happened to the anonymous sailors is still unknown to this day. Did the man just die of natural causes and pass away in the night, or was he a victim of foul play? Did the second man run away when he saw his companion lying dead on the floor, or was he actually responsible for the untimely death? This mystery will most likely never be solved, but there is one clue that remains that points to treachery. There have been dozens of sightings of a man dressed in eighteenth-century sailor's attire reported in the room next to the fireplace where the mystery man lay dead. Numerous White Horse Tavern employees over the years have had their own encounters with the somnolent specter and constantly report unexplained sightings of this man, as well as hearing footsteps from the second floor although no humans are actually walking upstairs above them. The footsteps are especially common around closing time and always emanate from the dead man's room, right around the large fireplace. The spirit seems to be very restless, almost pacing the floor where his death took place. Therein lies the clue to his demise. Parapsychologists who study ghosts and their earthy downfalls argue that murder victims will lie in wait for their assailants to return and exact their revenge. Most likely, this man was murdered, asphyxiated as he slept by his bunkmate. The murderer then stole his

This apparition of a murdered traveler lurks in the upstairs dining room of Newport's venerable White Horse Tavern. Is he waiting to exact revenge for a murder committed over 250 years ago? *Photo courtesy of the author.*

belongings and crept silently out of the house, never to be seen again. The dead man's spirit is lurking by the fireplace, waiting for his attacker to return.

So if you ever visit Newport and dine at the White Horse Tavern, remember: you might not be alone. But fear not, you have nothing to worry about unless you were the one who committed the crime. But also remember: ghosts of murder victims are patient; they have all of eternity to exact their revenge.

## CHAPTER 3

# THE BRITISH ARE...HERE!

The American Revolution was a long time coming, with colonial merchants evading British revenue agents and other various tax vehicles like the Sugar and Stamp Acts for many years. The colonial merchants essentially thumbed their noses at the British captains charged with collecting the tariffs that applied to the cargoes as they sailed their goods up and down Narragansett Bay. For many years, the British kept a presence in Newport Harbor, with a large man-of-war and other smaller support vessels patrolling the harbor and bay to ensure that the British Crown received the duties to which it was entitled. This game of cat and mouse lasted for the better part of the mid- and later eighteenth century, and usually the Newport merchants paid far less than they were supposed to contribute. While protesting the reviled Stamp Act of 1765, the locals resorted to a mob mentality and essentially stormed the home of tax collector Augustus Johnston with pitchforks and flaming torches. Johnston was so terrified that he hid in his cellar until the unruly gang passed, then quietly boarded the first ship for England the next morning and returned to London forever. Eventually, the Stamp Act was repealed.

The colonists wanted protection from the British Crown but were reluctant to assist in paying the bill for it. The British Treasury was all but bankrupted after fighting a lengthy and costly war with the French and their Native American allies from 1754 to 1763. The British did gain Canada and essentially all of the territory east of the Mississippi River, keeping the colonists safe from the French army, but at an expensive price. The British

Crown, with the imposition of various acts and tariffs, wanted the colonial merchants to help contribute to the war effort; however, the colonists were not very generous with their hard-earned money and were certainly not eager to turn it over without a fight.

One of the most reviled revenue collectors was Lieutenant William Duddingston, a proud Scotsman of the Royal Navy. Lieutenant Duddingston received his first command in Newport in 1772 aboard the twin-masted, eight-gun revenue cutter *Gaspee*. Duddingston, after arriving from Boston, knew full well of the Newport merchants' reluctance to pay their fair share of the war bill and was determined to get the Crown's due. To make matter worse, Duddingston looked on the colonists with disdain and was equally suspicious of the local customs agents in Newport, who might have occasionally looked the other way when a large cargo from an influential local merchant sailed into port. There was no question: Duddingston was there to do his job to the letter of the law, and friction was growing that would eventually explode into an all-out conflict. Typically in the past, small flat-bottomed boats, barges and ferries evading the British tariffs would just ignore the commands to yield from the revenue cutters and escape into small rivers or estuaries. However, with the arrival of Lieutenant Duddingston, these tactics were no longer effective. The brash young Duddingston would not be ignored by the coastal runners. He would fire warning shots over the boats, forcing the tax evaders to halt and be boarded and searched. The search of the vessels typically uncovered undeclared merchandise, which was immediate grounds for seizure of the goods and the boat itself. Local merchants had reached a boiling point with Duddingston and his tactics.

On June 8, 1772, Lieutenant Duddingston and the *Gaspee* were trailing a small coastal packet, the *Hannah*, that had departed from Newport en route to Providence. Captain Lindsey and the *Hannah* were very familiar with the coastal waters around Warwick Neck and the approach to Providence; Duddingston was not. At a small narrow bay called Namquit Point, the *Hannah* slid over a shallow sandbar and proceeded north to the safety of Providence. The *Gaspee* and its inexperienced crew missed the crossing point and were beached on a sandbar with the tide streaming out. The *Gaspee* was trapped until the next morning's inbound tide could free the boat from the sandy bottom. It was a sitting duck, and Lieutenant Duddingston knew it. Word quickly spread along the Providence waterfront, and an angry armed mob was rapidly gathering, planning to seek revenge against the hated ship and its captain.

That evening, just before midnight, the armed mob, with paint-smeared faces, rowed from Fenner's Wharf in Providence to exact their revenge on the ill-fated schooner. The mob, comprising many wealthy local merchants and businessmen who were fueled by rum punch, as well as a burning desire to destroy the *Gaspee*, rowed their longboats silently alongside the stranded ship, demanding its surrender. The de facto leader of the raiders was unscrupulous Providence merchant John Brown, who loudly declared himself the "Sheriff of Kent County" and ordered the immediate arrest of Lieutenant Duddingston. Duddingston, of course, rejected the raiders' offer and ordered his men to fire on anyone boarding the ship, but the drunken horde quickly overwhelmed the sleepy-eyed crew. Duddingston himself was shot through the leg during the mêlée but would survive. The *Gaspee*'s crew was stripped and placed in a rowboat and allowed to sail to the nearby shoreline. The victorious boarding party quickly ransacked the doomed ship, securing anything of value that could be carried off, and then set the flames that would start the American Revolution.

The *Gaspee* burned brightly throughout the night and into the early hours of the next morning—all the way to the waterline. The fuse was set, and the powder keg of a full-blown conflict was about to explode. The British were outraged that a band of hooligans would attack a Royal Navy ship and wound one of its captains. Rest assured, the British had long memories, and once war was declared, the Royal Navy would exact its revenge on an old nemesis: the port of Newport itself.

By 1774, Newport was estimated to be the fourth-wealthiest colonial city, and the British government knew it. After the *Gaspee* incident, the Royal Navy increased its patrols throughout Narragansett Bay and also increased its firepower in the area by sending the twenty-gun frigate HMS *Rose* to Newport Harbor as a sign that the Crown meant business. The British government wanted its tax money and wasn't going to take smuggling lightly. The British occupation of nearby Boston was a boon for Newport's economy. Most of the goods could not enter the northern port because of the British blockade, detouring more ships to offload their cargo along Newport's waterfront. But in March 1776, that would all change.

With recent battlefield losses in Lexington and Concord and the installation of rebel cannons overlooking Boston Harbor, the British commanders decided it was time to evacuate the city and relocate the bulk of naval operation to another port. A large garrison of British soldiers and sailors was sent to Staten Island, just south of Manhattan, to control New York Harbor and attack the rebel troops on Long Island in the summer of 1776. A second large garrison of six thousand men under the control of General Henry Clinton would soon find a home as well. Commanding General William Howe required a strategic port that could still be in proximity to Boston and northern New England, as well as control the passages to New York City along the eastern Long Island coastline. Newport was the perfect choice. The city met all of the Royal Navy's strategic requirements, and the British could exact revenge against the pesky Narragansett Bay merchants in one fell swoop. So, on December 8, 1776, a day that will live in local infamy, General Clinton, with eight British men-of-war and twenty ships of the line, along with dozens of transport vessels and roughly six thousand troops, landed in Newport without resistance. The British were here!

The occupation had begun, and Newport's golden age of commerce was over. The British immediately seized any large homes they wanted to garrison the men. General Clinton set up residence in the luxurious Banister Mansion on the corner of Spring and Pelham Streets, about two blocks from the waterfront. Newport's population was cut in half virtually overnight; anyone who was pro-Revolution fled the town for good. The Old Colony House, Rhode Island's seat of government and the site of the reading of the Declaration of Independence, was used to quarter troops as well, and the basement served as a stable. It would be an understatement to say that the British were not kind to Newport during their stay. During the occupation, the winters were extremely harsh, and the entire island was deforested for firewood. When the firewood ran out, homes were ripped apart board by board and burned to provide heat. It is estimated that the British destroyed upward of two hundred properties during their stay. Other homes were torn down, shipped to New York and reassembled there for Loyalists. The British soldiers also found time to take target practice in local graveyards, shooting holes through headstones with their muskets.

The British occupation would last almost three years and throw Newport into an economic slump from which it would never recover. Most of the population who fled north to Providence remained there after the war. The industrial revolution was taking shape in the northern part of the state, and employment would be easier to find there. Newport would never again regain its place as a wealthy and powerful colonial seaport town. When the British finally evacuated Newport in October 1779, the city was in shambles. The British no longer needed Newport's strategic location. The war effort had turned toward the southern colonies, and after exhausting all natural resources, the British no longer wanted to spend another frigid winter in Rhode Island. As one last goodbye, the British

*Above*: The massive landing fleet of the British navy arrives in Newport in December 1776. With over six thousand troops and eighty ships, the armada stretched almost a mile along the west side of Aquidneck Island. *Photo courtesy of the Naval Sea power Archive.*

*Right*: This gravestone in Newport's common burying ground still bears a scar from the British occupation. Along with shooting holes through headstones, the British army also deforested the area for firewood and then ripped apart houses board by board to keep warm. When it finally abandoned Newport in 1779, it left behind a city in ruins. *Photo courtesy of the author.*

burned several colonial structures, including the Beavertail Lighthouse, on their retreat. Thankfully, the venerable Trinity Church, a symbol of downtown Newport, was spared, most likely because the burning of an Anglican church would be considered sacrilegious.

A large French fleet commanded by General Rochambeau would use Newport as a base of operations in 1780 before departing southward in 1781 to assist General Washington in the British defeat at Yorktown, but the damage to Newport was done. The once-powerful and wealthy seaport was reduced to a struggling fishing port that would be mired in an economic downturn for decades.

Those people who view Newport as a snapshot of colonial life today regard the British occupation as a blessing in disguise. Had the British never occupied Newport, the city would have continued its progression as a powerful and influential coastal port. If the city had continued to prosper and been caught up in the industrial revolution, many, if not all, of Newport's colonial structures might have been deemed unnecessary and torn down, to be replaced by factory buildings and other modern structures. Progressing even further, Newport might have developed into a sprawling metropolis, just like its colonial brethren New York City, Boston or Philadelphia. Just imagine thirty-story high-rises or gridlocked avenues along the pristine harbor front. So for those of us who enjoy the colonial charm and the walks down three-hundred-year-old cobblestone streets, the British occupation was actually a godsend. Newport's enduring colonial feel and charm were essentially preserved by the occupation, although the city's growth was inevitably stunted forever.

# CHAPTER 4

# ALL'S FAIR IN LOVE AND WAR

As we explored in the last chapter, the occupying British army did irreparable damage to Newport. There is no question that the powers that be commanding the upstart rebel forces were keenly aware of how strategically important Newport was in the overall war effort and their struggle for freedom from the oppressive British Crown. It was not just Newport itself, but all of Aquidneck Island, which encompasses current-day Middletown and Portsmouth, as well as the vast inland waterway of Narragansett Bay. Numerous attempts during the Revolution to retake the island by combined Patriot and French forces were ultimately failures, and the British would remain in their floating fortress as long as they deemed it "strategically important."

That does not mean other efforts were not made to expedite the British departure, or at least agitate the command structure of the local adversaries in hopes that they would abandon Newport for good.

The most famous of these covert attacks was the attempted kidnapping of the commander of local British troops, General Richard Prescott. As outlandish as this scheme might sound, the rebels would actually be presented the opportunity, all because of the general's wandering eye and his desire to spend time with "a loyal British subject."

General Prescott was not the first general in charge of the occupying British army. The original invasion force was under the command of Sir Henry Clinton, who had a reputation for harboring severe disdain for the disloyal colonists. Prescott was much worse, with a reputation of outright hatred for his upstart colonial foes. He was also infamous for his harsh treatment of prisoners of war. Total destruction of this rebellion was General Prescott's ultimate goal.

In December 1776, just about the same time the British were landing in Newport, there was another setback for the rebellion. The most trusted general in George Washington's army was captured in New Jersey by the British after a night of, let's just say, merriment. General Charles Lee, second in command of the American army, was captured after a night of drinking at a local tavern, severely hampering George Washington's command structure. With the British securing General Lee in their stronghold of New York City, an armed raid to free the captured prisoner was out of the question. The only option was to exchange the general for a high-ranking British officer, which they did not have. One British commander quickly came to mind, however: Richard Prescott. This would not be the first time Prescott would be targeted for capture. He had surrendered to Patriot forces after the ill-fated defense of Quebec and was exchanged for Rhode Island Militia general John Sullivan in 1776. Could lightning strike the same man twice?

How could a British general be captured while surrounded by nearly six thousand troops and dozens of warships patrolling the bay? The rebels would need to catch him at a moment of weakness, when his guard was down. As it turns out, not all the soldiers were too enthralled with their pretentious commander. There was talk amongst the ranks that General Prescott would frequently make his way to the countryside to visit a wealthy Tory landowner and merchant named Henry Overing. (A Tory was a colonist opposed to the revolution.) While visiting his benefactor's farm, General Prescott was rumored to secretly sneak off with Mrs. Overing to engage in some extramarital adult activities. The rumors made their way to Providence, to Major William Barton of the Rhode Island Militia, that General Prescott might have a mistress on a farm just outside the heavily guarded downtown area. This was the break Barton needed, a chance to catch the general with his pants down, so to speak.

On July 9, 1777, Major Barton and his raiding party of about forty men, shoved off from Warwick Neck, making their way across Narragansett Bay in five longboats toward the farm, which is located on the modern-day Middletown/Portsmouth town line. The boats stealthily made their way across the darkened waterway with cloth-covered oars to muffle their sounds. They were extremely cautious not to alert the lookouts on the British warships to which they were passing perilously close. The men in Major Barton's raiding party were chosen specifically because of their knowledge of the bay, from years of navigating these waters under the cover of darkness in the attempt to smuggle goods past British tax collectors. When the marauders arrived at the farm, they discovered a lightly guarded manor house and quickly overpowered a lone sentry. As it turns out, General Prescott had such little respect for the rebels that he traveled with only a handful of aids and guards, never thinking his enemy would be daring enough to kidnap him. Just imagine the startled look on General Prescott's face when he was awakened by Major Barton's firearm staring him directly in the face. The general was tied, gagged and taken from the room so fast that he wasn't even permitted to dress. He was dragged half naked across the darkened farm fields and thrown into the bottom of one of the waiting longboats, which quickly rowed back to Providence before anyone in the house could be alerted.

The raid was a success. The Patriot army now had its high-level prisoner to exchange for General Charles Lee, and Major Barton and his men were hailed as heroes. Barton was promoted to lieutenant colonel, and his men would share a sizeable reward for their daring capture. Barton would continue to serve in the Rhode Island Militia, playing a key role in the attempted but unsuccessful recapture of Newport and Portsmouth during the Battle of Rhode Island in 1778. The local Revolutionary fort in Tiverton, Rhode Island, still bears his name as a tribute to his heroism.

In the spring of 1778, the two prisoners were exchanged. General Charles Lee would continue to fight for independence, serving General Washington at the Battle of Monmouth in New Jersey. Unfortunately for Lee, he was court-martialed after the battle for disregarding orders and disrespecting General Washington. After his dismissal from the army, Charles Lee retired to his farm in Virginia.

As for General Prescott, he returned to Newport to the smirks and grimaces of his troops and was replaced as commander by General Robert Pigot. Prescott did, however,

Lieutenant Colonel William Barton, commander of the Rhode Island Militia's raiding party that bravely kidnapped British general Richard Prescott. *Photo courtesy of Wikimedia commons.*

*Left*: General Charles Lee was captured outside a tavern in New Jersey by British soldiers after a night of heavy drinking. After being exchanged for British general Richard Prescott, Lee was kicked out of the American army for disobeying the orders of General George Washington. *Photo courtesy of Wikimedia commons.*

*Below*: Prescott Farm was the country estate of a wealthy British Tory named Henry Overing and the unlikely location of the kidnapping of General Prescott. The farm is currently owned by the Newport Restoration Society and is open to the public on a seasonal basis. *Photo courtesy of the author.*

remain in the army until the end of the war and fought valiantly during the Battle of Rhode Island, where he ironically faced his former captor, William Barton. The location of his capture is still referred to as Prescott Farm today; it is owned by the Newport Restoration Society, which offers seasonal tours of the grounds.

And what about Mrs. Overing? Was she in the bed when General Prescott was captured? Well, according to eyewitnesses in the raiding party, Prescott was alone in bed when he was captured. They go on to say that there was no evidence that Mrs. Overing was even at the farm at the time of the capture. Apparently, the only people on-site that evening included a handful of the general's staff, a guard and Mr. Overing and his son. So what to make of the rumored affair between the general and the lady of the manor? Perhaps the story was a cleverly crafted ruse by members of General Prescott's own army in an attempt to have their pompous and arrogant general removed from command. Whatever the source of the story, the final objective was achieved: General Prescott was captured and exchanged. And perhaps Mrs. Overing was just a way to add a little spice to the rumor mill; she will remain one of the American Revolution's unsolved mysteries.

## CHAPTER 5

# THE NOT-SO-FABULOUS PERRY BROTHERS

Almost every colonial town and city has its favorite native sons, heroes of battles and conquerors of hostile enemies on faraway shores. Newport is no exception, often singing the praises of local boys Oliver Hazard and Matthew Calbraith Perry, early champions of the fledgling U.S. Navy. But on closer examination, this naval duo's exploits might not have been so heroic after all.

The Perry brothers were not even born in Newport; both Oliver and Matthew were born to the west across Narragansett Bay in South Kingston, near the village of Wakefield—Oliver in 1785 and Matthew in 1794—to a navy father who served bravely during the American Revolution. At the young age of thirteen, the quick-tempered and strong-willed Oliver secured a midshipman's commission with the help of his well-connected father. Without his father's influence, it would have been nearly impossible for a thirteen-year-old to receive such a lofty position. He even served under his father's command aboard the frigate USS *General Greene* in a quasi war against France in 1799. For the next six years, Oliver Hazard Perry was an obscure midshipman serving on various missions, including quelling the Barbary pirates off the coast of Libya in Africa, but he was never involved in any notable skirmishes. In 1807, Perry was in charge of a small flotilla of gunboats along the Rhode Island and Connecticut coastlines, a duty he felt was both tedious and demeaning. In 1809, Oliver Hazard received his first oceangoing command aboard the fourteen-gun schooner *Revenge*.

Perry's luck steadily declined after receiving command of the *Revenge*. In June 1810, the schooner was severely damaged in a storm en route to Charleston, South Carolina. Perry's new assignment was off to a bad start, and to make matters worse, Perry became severely ill from the extreme heat and humidity of his new southern port of call. Perry's fragile health and weak foundation would always hinder his ability to command his ships. In early 1811, Perry was reassigned to northern waters to conduct surveys of the bays and harbors of the southern New England coastline, but his bad luck would follow him there as well. Later that year, while sailing through a heavy fog in western Block Island Sound, Perry's ship hit some offshore rocks and sank. The subsequent court-martial exonerated Perry, mostly because of his navy father and his influence, instead placing the blame on the clueless pilot, although Perry had assured his navigator that he was in safe waters. Perry took an extended leave of absence from the navy and got married in the meantime.

In May 1812, war broke out with Great Britain, and Perry was placed in command of a small fleet of gunboats in and around Newport Harbor. Once again agitated with a command he felt was pathetic, Perry pleaded with the navy for a high seas assignment. The navy complied, shipping Perry to the Great Lakes Squadron to oversee construction of a flotilla of gunboats. It was here where Perry would achieve his greatest military success, although the incident is mired in controversy. On September 10, 1813, Perry's squadron engaged a smaller, inferior British force. Perry's gunboat, despite facing a smaller force, was literally shot out from under him, and he was forced to abandon ship, grab his battle flag and swim to another boat, the *Niagara*. It was on the *Niagara* where Perry would achieve his greatest naval success, turning the tide of war on the Great Lakes by eventually defeating the British squadron and taking control of the strategically important area. Perry's message to then-president William Henry Harrison read, "We have met the enemy and they are ours," forever preserving Oliver Hazard Perry's legacy as an American naval hero. Thus, the spin doctors of the early nineteenth century anointed Oliver Hazard Perry a naval hero, even though he was constantly ill and complained endlessly about his lowly assignments, had a ship under his command sink in bad weather and had another ship blown to smithereens from under him by a smaller, inferior force. Perry certainly was the recipient of a positive public relations campaign, perhaps once again the lingering effects of having an influential navy dad.

In 1814, the newly anointed naval hero was promoted to full captain and given the honor of commanding a forty-four-gun frigate, the *Java*, under construction in Baltimore. The *Java*'s mission was to suppress pirate activity in the Mediterranean Sea and along the northern coast of Africa. Controversy would again follow Perry on his new mission. While anchored in Naples, Italy, Perry and marine commander John Heath engaged in a heated argument, which resulted in Perry slapping Heath across the face. Once again, Perry was court-martialed and given a minor reprimand, although Heath would take matters into his own hands. Upon the *Java*'s return to U.S. waters, Heath would challenge Perry to a duel, and the contest took place on the same field where Aaron Burr had been shot dead in a duel with Alexander Hamilton. The results of this match were quite different, however. Heath missed his shot at Perry, and Perry refused to pull the trigger, thus ending the feud without bloodshed and restoring his honor.

Perry's next assignment was a diplomatic mission to Venezuela in 1819, sailing down the Orinoco River to the then capital city of Angostura. This was a dangerous mission; the area was notorious for mosquitoes and yellow fever, which was usually fatal once contracted. Perry and his ship, the *Nonesuch*, arrived in the capital on July 27, 1819, and almost instantaneously twenty crewmen were stricken with yellow fever. Five of the crewmen would later perish from the dreaded disease of the tropics. Perry was particularly worried given his propensity for illness, but early on in the mission, his health was holding up in the harsh, humid conditions. On August 15, with the diplomatic mission concluded, Perry quickly weighed anchor and raised his sails. He rode the rapid currents of the Orinoco River north to the open and disease-free waters of the Atlantic Ocean, en route to Port of Spain in Trinidad. But two days later, Perry awoke abruptly with severe chills and a fever—he had contracted the deadly yellow fever.

With Perry's susceptibility to illness, his condition quickly deteriorated, and despite the efforts of the crew to quickly reach Port of Spain, Oliver Hazard Perry would die on his thirty-fourth birthday, August 23, 1819, just off the coast of Trinidad. Strangely enough, Perry's wife, Elizabeth, had dreamt the day before that her husband died but remarked, "If I were superstitious, the dream would worry me, but I am not and I shall think of it no more." Well, Elizabeth's nightmare was true, and Perry's body was quickly interred in Port of Spain, Trinidad, by the startled crew hoping to minimize the spread of the disease.

But Oliver Hazard Perry's body would not rest in peace. Just seven years after his death, his remains were exhumed and brought to Newport for an official military burial in the Common Burying Ground on the outskirts of town. Then, ten years later, in 1836, Perry's remains would again be relocated, this time to a family plot in the adjacent Island Cemetery. So even after his death, Oliver Hazard Perry was on the move; he was disinterred twice and buried three times in the span of seventeen years. A large granite obelisk given as a gift by the State of Rhode Island marks Perry's final resting place, and an impressive statue towers over Newport's Washington Square, inscribed with Perry's famous edict: "We have met the enemy and they are ours!" Newport's controversial naval hero was finally home to stay.

Oliver Hazard's little brother, Matthew Calbraith Perry, was certainly not as famous as his older brother, but one thing is for sure: he accomplished more militarily and was far more successful as a naval officer than his brother. Matthew was born in 1794 and was sailing on boats around Narragansett Bay from a very young age. In 1809, Matthew received his midshipman's commission and served aboard the USS *Revenge* under the command of his older brother. He also served in the U.S. Navy off the African coast, suppressing piracy and enforcing antislavery laws on the high seas. Matthew's first major command was aboard a twelve-gun sloop named the *Shark*. The *Shark* was ordered to take control of an important southern port, deemed to be the Gibraltar of the Gulf of Mexico. On March 22, 1822, Perry sailed into Key West Harbor and planted the American flag, literally claiming this strategic Florida harbor for the United States. The anti-piracy fleet was eventually headquartered in Key West under Captain David Porter, and the seaport was used to suppress piracy around Florida and the Caribbean.

In the early 1830s, Perry helped to establish the training programs at the U.S. Naval Academy using an apprentice system to mentor new seamen. Perry also established a navy gunnery school

One of Newport's naval heroes, Oliver Hazard Perry, is seen here transferring the command flag during the War of 1812's Battle of Lake Erie. Because of Perry's heroics, in which he captured a British squadron, he was one of America's most decorated officers in the early history of the U.S. Navy. *Photo courtesy of Wikimedia commons.*

off the coast of New Jersey, but his biggest contribution was the advancement of the U.S. Navy into the modern steam era. Perry realized that sail power was from a past age and, if the United States was to dominate the oceans of the world, a new propulsion system would be necessary to power the navy into a new era. Matthew C. Perry would now be known as the "Father of the Steam Navy."

In 1840, Perry was promoted to the rank of commodore and was given command of the Brooklyn Navy Yard. In the mid-1840s, he returned to the waters off the African coast to enforce antislavery laws. During the Mexican-American War, Perry successfully supported General Winfield Scott in the capture of the port of Veracruz by blockading the Mexican escape route from the sea. In July 1847, he attacked the Mexican city of Tabasco personally, leading a 1,173-man landing force and attacking the city from land. It was obvious that Perry's heroic actions impressed his superiors in Washington, D.C., when he was handed his next very important assignment. Perry was to open a closed society to the east by any means necessary.

In 1852, Perry sailed from Norfolk, Virginia, with four modern steam warships and a letter of request from U.S. president Millard Fillmore outlining exactly what the now powerful United States was essentially demanding from the mysterious society to the east. Arriving at the mouth of Uraga Bay near the city of Edo (modern-day Tokyo) on July 14, 1853, Perry's black-hulled steam vessels were initially denied entry by local government officials. However, Perry insisted that he had a letter of demand to deliver in person to the Japanese hierarchy and would not take no for an answer. The Japanese officials eventually relented when faced with the power of the United States' powerful armaments. The Japanese government might have also been persuaded to permit Perry to enter the city when he threatened to bombard the city relentlessly with the full force of his modern armada. Perry basically told the shoguns of Japan, "You have one year to comply with our list of requests or your city will become rubble. I will return in one year to ensure your compliance to President Fillmore's request."

With the letter delivered, Perry was off to explore the coast of China before returning to Japan in February 1854 to sign a treaty with the Japanese leaders, who were basically told take this offer or else. When Perry returned, he brought even more firepower to make sure the Japanese knew he meant business. Perry returned with eight naval vessels that so intimidated the locals that they referred to the steaming monsters just offshore as *Kurofune* or the "Black Ships." In all honesty, the antiquated Japanese defenses were no

The frightened Japanese called Matthew C. Perry's steamships Kurofune, or the "Black Ships," because of the thick, dark smoke pouring from their stacks. Commodore Perry was in Japan as an official representative of President Millard Fillmore. Perry's negotiating and subsequent treaty opened Japan to trade with the West. *Photo courtesy of Wikimedia commons.*

match for Perry's modern weaponry. He could have easily turned the local cities to dust.

When Perry signed the Treaty of Kanagawa as an official representative of the United States government, he was at the peak of his navy career. Perry's treaty created a vast new trading partner with the Empire of Japan and also secured a safe haven in the Far East for any disabled American ship and a safe port of call for any wayward sailor.

Perry returned to the United States in 1855 as a hero and the man who opened the Far East to trade with his diplomatic skills. It also didn't hurt to have a flotilla of warships at his disposal as an ace in the hole that could have easily pulverized his adversary into oblivion.

Perry was given a $20,000 grant by Congress and published a three-volume work about his exploits in the Land of the Rising Sun. Perry was also promoted to rear admiral and placed on the navy's retired list as a reward for his exemplary service to the United States. Perry was also in declining health from years of excessive drinking. Perry's lifestyle finally caught up with him in 1858, when he died in New York City from cirrhosis of the liver at the age of sixty-four. A few weeks after his death, Matthew Calbraith Perry's remains would be returned to Newport and buried in the prestigious Island Cemetery, not far from his older brother, Oliver Hazard.

Matthew C. Perry's legacy can still be felt today. Every summer in Newport, there is a cultural exchange with sister city Shimoda, Japan, called the Black Ships Festival commemorating the Treaty of Kanagawa and the new era of trade with the people of Japan. Many of the activities are held around Perry's statue as a tribute to a man who basically made Japan an offer it couldn't refuse. Perry's "take it or else" demands to the Japanese leaders forever changed the face of the modern American economy and ushered in the age of a truly global trade.

## CHAPTER 6

# THE MYSTERY OF THE
# *SEA BIRD*

Newport's very existence has always been linked to its deep and well-protected harbor and the vast Atlantic Ocean that lies just over its doorstep. This lively seaport was once the weigh station for all kinds of colonial cargo and post–Revolutionary War goods that had crisscrossed the mighty Atlantic, the treacherous Caribbean Sea and even the tranquil waters of Narragansett Bay to the north. Newport was such a busy and prosperous hub that it rivaled New York, Boston, Philadelphia and Charleston, South Carolina, in overall shipping volume and trading activity. So in May 1850, when the three-hundred-ton brigantine *Sea Bird* was seen on the horizon off Brenton's Point, it was on just another routine cargo voyage making its way to the docks to unload its freight.

The *Sea Bird* was returning from Honduras with a load of exotic hardwood, pitch pine and sacks of coffee. John Durham, a veteran New England sea captain from Middletown, Connecticut, was at the helm and had sailed this route numerous times. Yet something was not quite right with his approach toward the harbor. Instead of entering the wharf area, as if guided by an invisible hand, the *Sea Bird* veered east and then north toward Newport's Easton's Beach and ran aground on a sandbar just off shore. The captain could not have missed the harbor entrance because of fog or stormy conditions—it was a clear sunny day. Something must have gone horribly wrong for a veteran captain to miss his mark by such a wide margin. In the

1850s, Easton's beach had a small enclave of fisherman living close to the water, so they immediately rowed out to the beached *Sea Bird* to question the captain about what had gone awry.

But when the local fishermen boarded the sailing ship, much to their amazement, there was no captain to be found. As a matter of fact, there was no crew either; the only living creatures aboard the vessel were a dog and a cat, and they weren't talking. To make the situation even more bizarre, there was a boiling pot of coffee on the galley stove, and the table was set for the eight crew members. The smell of freshly lit tobacco still wafted through the crew quarters, indicating that humans had been aboard in the not-too-distant past.

The fishermen searched the captain's log for clues but found nothing to indicate the fate of the lost souls onboard. By all indications, the four-month voyage had gone smoothly, and Captain Durham's last entry was "Brenton's reef sighted," a sure sign that people had been on board very recently and that the captain was preparing to sail to the waterfront for the final leg of their journey. The navigational instruments were in place, and cash equaling about sixty dollars was in plain sight on the captain's desk—a definite clue that ruled out pirates and a high seas robbery. A small skiff was still lashed to the deck, which ruled out that the crew had abandoned ship on a life raft. Besides, the sails were still unfurled, flapping in the breeze, and the ship was in perfect condition. Another crew of a fishing schooner returned to Newport a short time later and reported passing the *Sea Bird* a few miles from shore. The fishing crew gave a wave to the *Sea Bird* and received a return gesture from Captain Durham, a sure indication that all was well aboard his ship. The captain gave no impression to the fishing crew that there were any signs of trouble.

Shortly after the *Sea Bird*'s beaching, a salvage crew arrived and began offloading the cargo, and attempts were made to refloat the ship off the sandbar that held it captive. The salvage crew's efforts were fruitless, and the *Sea Bird* remained trapped off the beach, still not yielding any clues to the whereabouts of the vanished crew. Whispers began to drift around the small fishing village and throughout Newport itself about the fortune of the lost souls. The fishermen had a remarkable and somewhat terrifying theory about the crew's disappearance—a seaman's legend passed down over two hundred years regarding the dark gray waters of the mysterious Atlantic Ocean. New England fishermen from Maine, Cape Cod and the entire Atlantic coastline had frequently reported sightings of sea serpents larger than a whale slithering along the coast.

Veteran sailors feared these murky waters because of these alleged sea serpents, which were capable of reaching up onto the decks and below into crew quarters and snatching helpless seamen to their watery graves. These creatures were so hideous and feared that some captains would alter their courses to avoid waters that had recently reported sightings of these lethal sea monsters. Most critics would argue that these stories are just old New England folklore and there is no basis for this bizarre conclusion to the crew's whereabouts. Realistically, however, there is no evidence to provide any clues regarding the fate of the men. No bodies were ever found, and no stranded sailor from the *Sea Bird* ever washed up on a nearby beach. The crew had literally vanished within sight of Newport. Did a giant sea creature from the depths snatch the defenseless men from their ship? No one will ever know, but one thing is for sure: a perfectly healthy crew and an experienced, veteran captain disappeared without a trace from a completely seaworthy sailing vessel, hours from the dock. That fact was irrefutable.

To make this tale even more astonishing, the next morning, a powerful coastal storm ravished the coastline throughout the day and into the night. The locals knew from experience that a stranded vessel trapped on a sandbar was doomed; the helpless *Sea Bird* would be mercilessly destroyed on the nearby rocks. As dawn broke the next day, locals headed to Easton's Beach expecting to see the vulnerable ship's remains broken

The eight-man crew disappeared from the *Sea Bird* just off the Newport Coast—was it possible they were snatched from the deck by a sea serpent? No trace of the crew was ever found, and the ship itself disappeared a few days after washing ashore at a local Newport Beach. *Photo courtesy of the author.*

and strewn across the sand. But to their utter amazement, the ship, like the crew, was gone. It was as if the *Sea Bird* had sailed out of Easton's Bay and back into the mighty Atlantic Ocean by the same invisible hand that had beached it on the sandbar in the first place. There was no wreckage to be found, no snapped masts against the rocky cliffs and no pieces of torn sail stretching across the wide beach. No trace of the stranded ship would ever be found, almost as if it were never there. The *Sea Bird*, like its doomed crew, was never seen again but remains to this day one of the most enduring maritime mysteries of this historic seaside community.

# CHAPTER 7

# THE ALMOST PRESIDENT FROM NEWPORT

There always seem to be strange yet subtle twists of fate that inevitably lead to something larger and more profound and, eventually, alter the course of history. Such was the case for a part-time Newport resident, a fanatical midwestern attorney and a president of the United States of America.

The part-time Newporter was a man named Levi P. Morton. If the name doesn't ring a bell, don't feel too badly. Morton was basically a footnote in late nineteenth-century political history. There is one small detail of Morton's political career that is noteworthy, however. He would make a decision that would eventually cost one president his life while at the same time denying himself the highest office in the land. Alas, if only hindsight were twenty-twenty.

Our tale of ironic twists begins with the election of 1880, with Republican James Garfield of Ohio running against Democratic nominee, Civil War general Winfield Scott Hancock. Garfield also served as a major general for the Union army and after the war would serve nine consecutive terms as a representative from the state of Ohio. The presidency was hotly contested after the incumbent, Rutherford B. Hayes, actually kept a campaign promise and served only one term as president. The 1880 election was the closest in U.S. history. Garfield collected a mere two thousand more popular votes than his political rival, Hancock, yet the majority of the Electoral College votes, easily becoming the twentieth president of our great nation.

At this point, you are probably wondering how Levi P. Morton, a man who wasn't even involved in the election, altered the course of presidential history. Morton turned down the offer to be Garfield's vice president, insisting instead on being appointed the United States minister to France (a similar position to today's ambassador). By accepting this position, Morton would infuriate a man who felt it was his "divine calling" to be chosen as minister to France. This man would soon make his feelings known to President Garfield that this snub was unforgivable and against the wishes of God Almighty himself. And he would not be denied revenge. This man's name was Charles Guiteau.

It's not that Levi P. Morton wasn't qualified for the job—quite to the contrary. Morton had an extensive political background, serving as a representative in Congress and honorary commissioner of the Paris Exhibition of 1878, in addition to being a successful dry goods merchant and banker in New York City. As a matter of fact, it was his time in Paris during the exhibition that really got him interested in the minister position, inevitably refusing the vice presidency. And being a successful politician and businessman from New York City meant Levi P. Morton would spend his summers where all of high society flaunted its wealth on the grandest scale: Newport, Rhode Island.

How Charles Guiteau came to the conclusion that the minister to France position was his by "divine right" was downright bizarre. In the summer of 1880, Guiteau was a passenger on a steamship that collided with another vessel in a heavy fog. Guiteau's steamship was able to safely return to port, while the other ship burned to the water line. To a demented Charles Guiteau, this was a sign from God that his life was spared to serve a greater purpose. He openly campaigned for Ulysses Grant to return to the presidency and then quickly switched allegiance when Garfield secured the nomination. After the election, which in his mind he won single-handedly for Garfield, Guiteau would arrive at the White House and plead his case for his divine position in Paris. Of course, the administration would have no part in this lunacy, and Guiteau was quickly dismissed. Guiteau's daily visits would continue even after the position was filled, and his petitioning became so annoying that he was finally told by Secretary of State James Blaine to leave the premises and never return.

At this point, Guiteau finally got the hint—and he was livid, to say the least. He borrowed fifteen dollars to purchase a large-caliber revolver and began to stalk the president. Guiteau's opportunity came at the now demolished Baltimore and Potomac Railroad station in Washington, D.C. President Garfield was on his way to visit his wife at a beach resort in Long Branch, New Jersey, when a demented Guiteau stepped out of the shadows and fired

This picture depicts President Garfield moments after he was fatally shot by deranged assassin Charles Guiteau at a train station in Washington, D.C. Guiteau was upset at the president for not appointing him as trade minister to France. That position went to prominent Newporter Levi P. Morton, who was offered the vice presidency but turned it down. Had he accepted, Morton would have become president after Garfield's death. *Photo courtesy of Wikimedia commons.*

two shots into the back of the president. The shots hit Garfield but missed the spinal column, so from early appearances, the wounds seemed minor. The would-be assassin was quickly subdued by bystanders and whisked away by police, all the while shouting loudly at the crowd, "I am a stalwart of the stalwarts now!" and "Arthur is president!"

But Arthur wasn't president yet because Garfield was still alive and appeared to be recovering nicely from his wounds. However, infections—probably caused by the unwashed hands of Garfield's physicians, as well as unsanitary medical devices—would eventually claim the president's life. On September 19, 1881, eleven weeks after the assassination attempt, President Garfield died. And Charles Guiteau was officially charged with killing the president. Guiteau's reaction was almost comical when hearing the charges against him: "The doctors killed Garfield, I just shot him."

However, the trial would go on in an almost circus-like atmosphere, in which Guiteau insisted on defending himself. He constantly berated the judge, the jury, the prosecution and his defense team. He answered his cross-examination questions in lengthy epic poems. He dictated an autobiography to the *New York Times* and ended his tale with a wanted ad for a good Christian woman. Guiteau even wrote letters to president Chester A. Arthur asking for his release because, as he pointed out, without his shooting President Garfield, Arthur would still be vice president. In the end, all of these bizarre defenses failed, and Charles Guiteau would be sentenced to death by hanging. Even up to the end, Guiteau was delirious, planning a speaking tour and even to run for president himself in 1884, when the pardon he was expecting was to be delivered. Guiteau seemed to enjoy the attention he was receiving, dancing his way to the gallows and reciting a long epic poem before he was hanged on June 30, 1882, almost one year after shooting President Garfield.

Alas, no pardon was received. And a president was dead, along with a deranged assassin who believed until his last moments on earth that he was destined to be minister to France. So what became of the "Almost President from Newport?" As it turned out, Levi P. Morton was actually a qualified and successful representative of the United States in Paris. Diplomatically, relations went quite smoothly with France during Morton's tenure, even improving to the point where the French became one of America's leading trade partners. Morton would eventually fulfill his destiny and become vice President on the ticket with President Benjamin Harrison in 1899. Morton's legacy is still felt in Newport today, even after his death in 1927. As a successful politician and businessman, Morton owned a large estate in Newport—Fairlawn—which eventually would be donated to Salve Regina University for use as a conference center. Another piece of property once used as a polo field was donated to the City of Newport and is currently a city park. Other property once owned by Morton in Hanover, New Hampshire, became the campus of Dartmouth College. So Levi P. Morton left a legacy in Washington, D.C., as well as Newport, but will probably be most remembered for a decision that changed the face, literally, of U.S. presidential history.

## CHAPTER 8

# WAS SHE WORTH
# $50 MILLION?

Marriage is a big commitment for most people, but for one Newport bachelor, his decision to marry a certain woman was extremely costly. Just how costly is the question, and the estimates are shocking. This bad decision caused this gentleman upward of $50 million. Who was this unfortunate love-struck young man?

His name was Cornelius Vanderbilt III, or Neily to close family and friends. Neily was the second-oldest son of Cornelius Vanderbilt II, chairman of the New York Central Railroad and head of the richest family in America at the time, and his wife, Alice. The young man had it all—a Yale education and a beautiful summer home, The Breakers—and would one day share in the massive railroad fortune. Neily's downfall might have started in 1892, when his beloved older brother, William Henry Vanderbilt II, died of typhoid fever at Yale University. Billy was the pride of the family—smart, extremely handsome and the one-day heir to the Vanderbilt throne. Sadly, all the money in the world and the most renowned physicians of the day couldn't save the young lad from his premature demise. The next king of Vanderbilt was gone.

Neily was much different from his older brother, often sickly with bouts of rheumatism and extremely quiet. Billy was considered the business brains of the next generation of Vanderbilt men, while Neily's passion was science and engineering. Neily was fascinated by figuring out inventions and how things worked. During the summer of 1895, Neily's world would be changed forever when, in the summer of 1895, the naïve young Vanderbilt courted a beautiful, yet spoiled, southern social climber named Grace Wilson.

Grace Wilson's father, Richard, had made a small fortune as a Civil War profiteer and had moved his family to New York City from Georgia at the outbreak of the Civil War. With his sizeable nest egg, Richard Wilson became a prominent banker and also dabbled in railroad investing. He certainly treated young Grace like a pampered princess, and she expected the best all the time. There is no question that the Wilsons were very well-to-do for their day but certainly nowhere near the massive wealth of the Vanderbilt family, who were by far in a league of their own. Grace Wilson had her eye on bigger game; she wanted to marry into a socially prominent family, and there was none bigger than the railroad clan.

Grace was no stranger to New York's high society. Her sister May had married Ogden Goelet, an heir to a large Manhattan real estate fortune. Grace was also very familiar with the inner workings of the Vanderbilt family; she had been secretly engaged to former heir-in-waiting, Billy, before his untimely death at Yale in 1892.

Neily's infatuation with Grace started in the summer of 1895, and the pair was inseparable during Newport's summer season as the young, love-drunk lad escorted his older mistress to all the top social events around the City by the Sea. The highlight of the summer season in 1895 was the grand opening of the Vanderbilt family's seaside mansion, The Breakers, on August 14. This evening had double significance: The Breakers' unveiling would also be the stage for Neily's sister Gertrude's debutante introduction to high society. When Neily attended this significant social outing with Grace Wilson, this was a troubling sign to his parents that Neily's infatuation was developing into more than a crush, and certainly marriage would be on the horizon. Alice Vanderbilt's worst fears were confirmed when Grace was Neily's date for the gala occasion and the smitten couple danced the night away cheek-to-cheek.

There was no mistaking Grace's charming southern beauty, with her striking hazel eyes, smooth complexion and silky auburn hair. Looks were not the reason Alice and Cornelius were so adamant their son was making a horrible mistake. They knew a gold digger when they saw one, and Grace Wilson was one of the most aggressive. She was once engaged to Cecil Baring, the son of Lord Revelstoke, but broke it off when he lost his fortune after the stock market crash of 1893. This was a sure sign to the Vanderbilts that Grace Wilson wanted only one thing: money. She was also notorious among high society in New York for chasing Jack Astor all around town, but to no avail. Grace now had her hooks in a bigger prize: Cornelius Vanderbilt III.

Besides the fact that Grace Wilson was six years older than her newfound love, there were other reasons the Vanderbilts were so against their son's new sweetheart. Alice Vanderbilt felt Grace was a little too worldly and adventuress, which was a polite way of saying she was much too sexually knowledgeable for the inexperienced Neily. Essentially, to Mrs. Vanderbilt, Grace had been around a little too much for her liking. Grace's family also had a couple strikes against it that didn't sit well with the house of Vanderbilt. Grace's father had made a tidy sum of money as a Civil War profiteer by selling supplies to the Confederate army, as well as running cotton through the Union blockade to England. With his ill-gotten profit, Mr. Wilson then started buying up Southern railroads that had been devastated during the Civil War. To high society, or at least in the eyes of the only family that truly

Grace Wilson captured the heart of railroad heir Cornelius Vanderbilt III. Vanderbilt went against his parents' wishes and married Miss Wilson, which got him disinherited, costing him $50 million. *Photo courtesy of Wikimedia commons.*

mattered, this was not an honorable way to make a fortune.

Neily's parents had an idea that they were sure would solve their dilemma. In November 1895, young Neily would be sent on a grand tour of Europe and the Near East, which they hoped would cure their young son of his lovesickness. The Vanderbilts' plan would ultimately backfire when Grace secretly met Neily in Paris, and the couple would soon become officially engaged. Cornelius was furious with his son and sailed to Europe himself in early 1896 to personally escort Neily back to New York City. The patriarch of the richest family in America also had a warning to the heir apparent: if you decide to go through with this union against my wishes, you will be disinherited from the Vanderbilt fortune.

On July 17, 1896, father and son had a heated shouting match over the pending nuptials, when the elder Cornelius suffered a massive stroke that slurred his speech and paralyzed the right side of his body. Immediately, the family placed the blame for the stroke squarely on Neily and the stress he had caused his father by disregarding his wishes. But stroke or no stroke, Neily was going to marry the woman he loved, and it didn't matter to the lovesick young man if he was forfeiting the tidy sum of $100 million. The wedding would proceed.

So despite the Vanderbilt family's wishes, Cornelius Vanderbilt III and Grace Wilson were married on August 3, 1896, in the parlor of Richard Wilson's New York City home without a Vanderbilt in sight. As a matter of fact, Neily was almost instantly shunned and ostracized by his wealthy and powerful family. When Neily's sister Gertrude wed Harry Paine Whitney on August 25, 1896, at The Breakers mansion, Neily and Grace were not invited. The family was backing up their threat to write Neily out of the clan and out of the will. Reality was starting to set in, and the newlyweds needed to reestablish a relationship with the deep-pocketed family. They could barely live on the annual $30,000 that their combined trust funds were paying them. However, the recuperating Cornelius Vanderbilt II had made it clear to relatives and friends: Neily was out of his life forever.

When Grace had her first child on April 30, 1898, there was some hope that the hardened grandparents would ease their stance a little and welcome the new Vanderbilt, Cornelius IV, into their lives. However, the opposite effect took place as the frail Cornelius II and Alice sailed for Europe for some rest and relaxation. In a correspondence with a friend, Alice refereed to the newborn as "that Wilson baby."

Neily, who was still employed as an engineer at the New York Central Railroad, concentrated on his work and implemented a new firebox on all the company's locomotives. This new firebox would reduce engine repairs and save the company thousands of dollars in repairs. If the young man couldn't win his father's love with his choice of a wife, at least he could gain his respect as a railroad engineer. Yet despite this new moneysaving device, Neily never got a word of thanks from his ailing father.

On September 11, 1899, Cornelius Vanderbilt II felt well enough to leave his seaside mansion to travel to New York City to attend a board of directors meeting for the New York Central Railroad. However, about halfway on the journey aboard his private rail car, the head of the Vanderbilt family suffered a cerebral hemorrhage and died at the age of fifty-six. All of his children were summoned to the Fifth Avenue mansion to be with their mother, so Neily, along with brother Reginald and sister Gertrude, took a private rail car to Manhattan to be with her. This was the first time in more than three years, since the defiant nuptials, that Neily was reunited with his family. But they would have to wait until brother Alfred returned from a graduation trip in Europe for the all-important reading of the will.

Late in October, the family assembled at The Breakers to learn their fate and to see if Cornelius II's warning was real or just an idle threat. When everyone was assembled, the Vanderbilt senior attorney read through the will and allocated the richest man in America's worldly possessions. Wife Alice received the Fifth Avenue residence, The Breakers mansion and a $7 million trust fund. Gertrude, Alfred, Reginald and youngest daughter Gladys all shared the income from a $20 million trust fund. Throughout the endless clauses and pages, Neily had yet to be mentioned. However, there was an ominous sign for his future inheritance. A gold medallion, which had been given to Commodore Vanderbilt for his gift of the SS *Vanderbilt* to the Union during the Civil War, was bequeathed to Neily's brother Alfred. The medallion was always passed to the next head of the Vanderbilt family. Neily's worst fears were finally realized when the ninth clause of the will was read: "To Cornelius Vanderbilt the III, I leave the income from a 1 million dollar trust fund and a gift of $500,000 outright."

With that clause, the remaining $42,575,000 of the estate was transferred to the new head of the Vanderbilts: Neily's younger brother Alfred. The will was dated July 18, 1896, the original date of Neily's pending wedding to Grace Wilson. The wedding had been postponed until August because of Neily's recurring rheumatism, but family patriarch Cornelius had made up his mind. Neily had defied his father's orders, and therefore his threat was real. Neily was out of the will and certainly out of the big money.

Perhaps the Vanderbilt family fortune was cursed after all. All those riches couldn't save Alfred Vanderbilt when the *Lusitania* was torpedoed off the coast of Ireland on May 7, 1915. Alfred was one of the 1,198 victims when the luxury liner sank in just eighteen minutes, within sight of the coastline. With all the time Alfred spent at the beach as a youngster, he had never learned to swim, and despite a hefty reward, his body was never recovered.

Now what was Neily to do? He was written off from the world's wealthiest family and still had a wife who was spending money at an alarming rate. Grace was entertaining high society like there was no limit to their wealth. Brother Alfred, the new head of the family, had smartly offered his older brother $6 million not to litigate the newly read will and save the family more embarrassment in the court of public opinion. However, from that day forward, the relationship between the brothers remained strained at best, and they never spoke again. Even when passing in public, they would not speak; they would only acknowledge each other with an icy nod. The very day Alfred assumed his job as head of the New York Central Railroad, Neily walked out of his office, never to return.

Neily spent most of his time tinkering and patenting new inventions. He also consulted with financier August Belmont on the construction of the New York subway system. Neily even tagged along on one of the early Wright brother flights in Kitty Hawk, North Carolina. Neily might not have been a super wealthy man, but the Vanderbilt name still carried plenty of currency. The same could be said for Grace. She still entertained like she was the head of high society and strived for the crown of "*the* Mrs. Vanderbilt."

Grace's first triumph over other society matrons occurred in 1902, when the German royal yacht docked in New York Harbor with Prince Henry aboard. Everyone who was anyone expected the Kaiser's brother to attend the Metropolitan Opera with Mrs. Astor, the reigning queen of high society. People were absolutely stunned when the young prince chose to attend the evening performance with the upstart Mrs. Grace Vanderbilt, a sure sign her place in society was for real.

That same summer in Newport, Grace pulled another coup that was certainly thought to be impossible. She was able to get the cast of the most popular play on Broadway, *Wild Rose*, to perform two nights at her Bellevue Avenue mansion, Beaulieu. These plays were considered, by all who attended, to be the highlight of the 1902 summer season. In another masterful stroke of Grace's marketing genius, she convinced husband Neily to build a 279-foot steam yacht christened the *North Star* and travel to Europe to hold court with every royal family they could. When photos of these regal trips hit the papers, they made the young couple look like ambassadors of America and the Vanderbilt family. Grace knew that sometimes perception can be more powerful than reality.

After Mrs. Astor passed away in 1906, Grace Wilson Vanderbilt ascended to the throne of New York and Newport society. There was one slight difference between the current and former queen, however. Mrs. Astor had a seemingly unlimited bankroll to fund her entertaining, while

Grace was squeaking by on the income of some mediocre trust funds. She had to cut corners whenever possible, like renting the Newport mansion, Beaulieu, as well as the furnishings, including the grand piano. Even the potted plants, linens, candlesticks, bath towels and crystal were all rented for the summer season. This generation of Vanderbilts was much different than earlier ones; the perception of wealth was largely an illusion. The $1 million Neily had inherited from his uncle George of the Biltmore in 1914, as well as a Fifth Avenue mansion, certainly helped Grace carry on her grand fantasy. Neily would also sell his inventions, especially those designed for railroads, to visiting dignitaries and businessmen while entertaining on his yacht, *North Star*. He needed to raise as much cash as he could for his free-spending wife, who was referred to in the society press as "Her Grace." When the press was less flattering, it dubbed her "the Kingfisher" for her endless pursuit of royalty.

With a new Fifth Avenue mansion at her disposal, Her Grace took her entertaining to an unprecedented level. Her guest lists included Mark Twain, former presidents Herbert Hoover and Theodore Roosevelt and prominent New Yorkers J.P. Morgan and John Jacob Astor. She also hosted countless dukes, duchesses, princes, princesses and royal heads of state from all over the world. The one guest who was rarely present at these elaborate functions was her husband. He preferred to tinker with his inventions in his soundproof laboratory while Grace entertained her guests. It was becoming strikingly clear that the couple had very little in common. Neily was quiet and preferred solitude, while Grace was his exact opposite—extremely extroverted and wanting the spotlight perpetually. They also had a different circle of friends who were not compatible socially. Grace never drank, while Neily consumed alcohol almost constantly and smoked three to four packs of cigarettes a day. Perhaps the pressure of being married to Her Grace was finally taking its toll. Or perhaps the wishes of his father constantly echoed through Neily's head. For whatever reason, the bickering became more pronounced, and the couple was now constantly fighting. Grace expected her husband to be at her side as a gracious host during her endless entertaining, while he preferred spending time at his New York private clubs or aboard his yacht. Neily had donated his beloved yacht, *North Star*, to the U.S. military for use during World War I. He had picked up another yacht, the *Winchester*, on which he started spending considerably more time. Grace grew suspicious and started reading his mail and listening to his phone calls. Neily finally had to install private phone lines and even built a small hidden elevator in his Fifth Avenue mansion as kind of an escape pod so he could secretly exit the house and stealthily escape from Grace. The woman with whom Neily had once been madly in love was now driving him crazy. Close friends would ask him why he didn't just get a divorce, and Neily would reply, "People in our position don't get divorced."

When Alice of The Breakers died in 1934, Grace Vanderbilt became the only "Mrs. Vanderbilt" and continued spending money and entertaining on Fifth Avenue, almost oblivious to the world around her. The Depression had been raging for years, and the world outside the mansion had become a commercial district, no longer a fashionable address to host globetrotting dignitaries. But Grace Vanderbilt hardly seemed to notice; she kept on living her gilded fairy tale. Grace was now sixty-one years old, and her striking good looks were gone. She had also gained a considerable amount of weight from all the fancy French dinners she threw for her acquaintances, and the charming young southern belle for whom Neily had fallen was gone. So was Neily. He essentially moved out of the house—permanently.

It was 1940, and the neighborhood had been transformed into skyscrapers and high-end retail stores, no longer a millionaires' row of Vanderbilt mansions. Neily finally sold the Fifth Avenue mansion for a paltry $1.5 million—much less than the $9 million he had been offered for the property just a few years earlier as the possible location for Rockefeller Center. It seems Grace had ordered Neily to turn down the deal—not the first time she had cost him a tidy sum of money. This time, Neily had no choice. He needed the cash to pay the mooring fees for his yacht, now docked in Miami, while his estranged wife continued to live the high life in Manhattan and Newport. There was also a stipulation that when the last great Vanderbilt mansion was sold, Grace could live there until one year after his death.

The fateful day came on March 2, 1942, when sixty-nine-year-old Cornelius Vanderbilt III died of a cerebral hemorrhage, the same condition that had claimed his father. Only his sister Gertrude made it to Florida to be by his side; Grace was nowhere to be found. The only thing she was concerned with was maintaining her schedule of luncheons, dinner parties and balls. She finally moved out of the mansion in 1945, and by 1947, any trace of the last citadel of grand entertaining on Fifth Avenue was gone.

Grace Wilson Vanderbilt would eventually pass away on January 7, 1953, at the age of eighty-three, and with her death, a bizarre chapter in American history called the Gilded Age was closed forever. Grace was the last link to an untamed period of lavish spending, . unimaginable fortunes and parties that could only be described as fantasies. Gone were the rows of mansions, the giant motor yachts, the liveried footmen and the fancy dress balls that lasted into all hours of the night. It almost seemed too good to be true—like a fairy tale for a handful of very wealthy, elite families. Just like the New York Central Railroad and the Vanderbilt fortune itself, it was all gone in the blink of an eye, as if it had almost never happened. As for Neily Vanderbilt, one must wonder how often he wished his nightmare marriage, the one strictly forbidden by his parents,

If he were able to do it over, it is unlikely Cornelius Vanderbilt III would have married Grace Wilson. It turned out his parents were correct, and Miss Wilson caused him a lifetime of misery and cost him his share of the family fortune. Would you marry this woman for $50 million? *Photo courtesy of Wikimedia commons.*

had just been one bad dream. But like the Gilded Age, his marriage was real, and he probably rued the day he made his $50 million mistake.

# CHAPTER 9

# THE GERMANS ARE
# HERE TOO?

Imagine that one day you are sitting on a bench in downtown Newport, enjoying the views of picturesque Newport Harbor, when all of a sudden an enemy submarine pops up out of the water. Well, you don't have to imagine too hard because this very event actually occurred in Newport on October 7, 1916, less than a year before the United States went to war with the Germans. Keep in mind that this was also one year after a German U-boat torpedoed the unarmed cruise ship *Lusitania* just south of the Irish coast. Needless to say, tension was building for war against the unpopular Germans.

Whatever the feelings were toward the German navy that October day in Newport, their *U-53* submarine was in port under the command of Captain Hans Rose to pay a social call to admirals at the Newport Navy Base. Since the United States had not officially entered the war on either side, Newport was officially neutral, and all ships were allowed a short period to dock and purchase supplies if necessary, even if they were at war. Two local admirals were given courtesy tours of the *U-53*, and Admiral Gleaves even brought his wife and daughter onboard to show them the interior of the vessel despite the fact that war with these men was less than a year away. A young ensign from the naval station named David Bagley was also welcomed onboard and had a pleasant exchange with Captain Rose, a meeting that would inevitably change Bagley's fate forever.

During the *U-53*'s short visit, U.S. government officials were scrambling to determine how to handle this unexpected visit from a somewhat hostile future enemy. When the Newport harbor master suggested the crew of the *U-53* might have to be quarantined, Captain Rose decided the good tidings should come to an end, and it was once again time for war. Rose's visit might have been more than just a social call to exchange pleasantries with the local navy brass; he did send a secret transmission to the imperial German high command before he departed. The *U-53* wreaked havoc off the coast of Nantucket for the next few days, sinking six merchant vessels bound for England. Thankfully, there was no loss of life during these sinkings—war was much more chivalrous in those days, and Captain Rose had a reputation for showing some compassion to his enemies. After the Germans boarded a merchant ship and discovered war materiel, the sailors were allowed to abandon ship before torpedoes were fired into the side of the now crewless vessel. Any ships that Captain Rose boarded and found to be strictly civilian in nature he allowed to pass unscathed. Captain Rose's journey was now complete; he was out of torpedoes, so he headed east for the German coast and awaited his next assignment and a fateful meeting with a new acquaintance.

With pressure mounting to join the war effort on the British side, Congress voted to enter World War I on April 6, 1917, and America wasted no time sending arms and men to aid its beleaguered ally. One of the ways the United States assisted the British was with increased patrols off the coast, hunting for enemy U-boats that might be prowling the British coastline. The destroyer *Jacob Jones* and its newly named captain, David Bagley, formerly of Newport Navy Base, had escorted a convoy of merchant vessels to France and were returning to their homeport of Queenstown, Ireland, when they had a fateful encounter.

December 6, 1917, was a day Captain David Bagley would always remember. The German *U-53* was in the area and spotted the *Jacob Jones* from a considerable distance. Despite the long distance of over eight hundred yards, the *Jacob Jones* was hit dead-on by the enemy torpedo and sank in only eight minutes, too rapidly for the ill-fated vessel to issue a distress call. Because the *Jacob Jones* had departed alone, no other allied ships knew their location, and with the frigid Atlantic and the exploding depth charges from the deck of the destroyer, two officers and sixty-four men would perish in the sinking. The *Jacob Jones* had the distinction of becoming the first American warship lost in combat during World War I.

About thirty minutes after the sinking, the *U-53* surfaced, and Captain Rose lived up to his humanitarian reputation. The enemy captain took two seriously wounded American sailors onboard to administer medical care. After submerging, Captain Rose was surveying the damage through his periscope when he recognized a familiar face floating in one of the lifeboats. It was the young navy ensign, David Bagley, whom he had recently encountered on his short visit to Newport only a few months before. In an almost inconceivable gesture, Captain Rose, breaking every military protocol and even placing his own ship and crew in danger, radioed the Queenstown base to report the location of the survivors of the *Jacob Jones*. Without this gesture of friendship in a time of war, the survivors of the torpedoed American destroyer would have certainly perished in the frigid waters of the Atlantic. Captain Bagley would be awarded the navy's Distinguished Service Medal for his handling of the disaster, as well as saving many of his crew—of course, with a small assist from Captain Rose.

Captain Bagley would remain in the navy through the end of the war and also served in World War II as a battleship commander. He eventually made it through the navy ranks to retire as an admiral. Captain Hans Rose of the *U-53* was one of the most prolific aces of submarine warfare, sinking thousands of allied ships. Yet Captain Rose would also be remembered as a humanitarian as well as a warrior—somewhat ironic in a time of war. It is doubtful that any other U-boat captain would remain in the area of a sunken enemy vessel until all the survivors were rescued and even throw food to the vanquished enemy so the men could remain alive until help arrived. Admiral Bagley would probably agree that this chance encounter with a soon-to-be-enemy captain on an October day in 1916 in Newport was a bizarre twist of fate. Yet this strange encounter would help save his life.

The German *U-53* suddenly appeared in Newport Harbor in 1916. Because the United States was not yet at war with Germany, the captain and crew were received cordially by local navy officials. After departing Newport, the *U-53* sank several merchant ships off the coast of Nantucket. *Photo courtesy of Wikimedia commons.*

# CHAPTER 10

# THE LADIES OF NEWPORT

Sometimes truth is stranger than fiction. Believe it or not, there was a scandal in Newport so outrageous and revolting at its time that it shook the very hierarchy of the United States Navy. This indignity was so appalling that it rocked the navy's chain of command all the way up to then assistant secretary of the navy and future president Franklin D. Roosevelt. To make this atrocity even more heinous, the investigation of the scandal was brought about by a sailor who had found the actions of a few of his comrades in arms even more unspeakable and outrageous than what he had witnessed previously at the San Francisco Navy Base.

San Francisco was the place to be at this time because it was about as wild as it got in the navy, especially if you happened to be gay. But for one sailor, Newport was even more flamboyant and shocking than anyone could have imagined, and an undercover investigation was launched that revealed secrets that were so unspeakable, they would be considered unbelievable today but were even more so in 1919.

During the First World War, Newport was home to roughly two thousand or so sailors and seamen, but at the end of the War to End All Wars, that number swelled to over twenty thousand. That's a huge number of frisky sailors in one little town. Newport was a place where sailors could easily find liquor, cocaine and a large number of brothels and tattoo parlors spread out throughout the seedy waterfront district. But one navy man found the gay activity at the Newport Navy Base so alarming that he notified his superiors of the shenanigans he witnessed.

It seems that Chief Machinist Mate Ervin Arnold was fairly homophobic and, while being treated for a severe case of rheumatism, witnessed some things he did not care for. While in the naval training hospital, Arnold overheard numerous conversations involving an effeminate young sailor named Samuel Rogers, who had a bit of a reputation among his peers as being a "pogue" around town. (Apparently, a "pogue" is a gay gentleman who prefers to play the traditionally feminine role, to put it politely.) Arnold also encountered another patient who gave him names and details of the sexual acts between the navy men and local gay men, as well as their meeting location: an apartment on Golden Hill Street in downtown. After Arnold was released from his hospital visit, he became obsessed with gathering information about these trysts and the effeminate sailors who dressed in drag, commonly known as the "Ladies of Newport." Chief Machinist Mate Arnold also uncovered that the downtown Army and Navy YMCA was a hotbed of gay activity, with the Episcopal military chaplain, the Reverend Samuel Neal Kent, acting as the master of ceremonies. It seems the Reverend Kent was notorious for paying young sailors for their companionship.

With this information in hand, Arnold brought his findings to his station commander, who then passed them along to his superiors. The results were disturbing enough to trigger an investigation to study the "immoral conditions" in Newport. Assistant Secretary of the Navy Franklin D. Roosevelt agreed that "a most searching and rigid investigation" needed to be conducted with the aim of prosecuting those individuals responsible for the "spread of degeneracy." The tactics the navy used to uncover the scandal were almost as astonishing as the sexual acts being committed. But FDR wanted to leave no doubt about the extent and depth of the sinful actions being committed at Newport Navy Base. The results of this investigation would leave no doubt whatsoever.

The navy's plan was to send straight sailors into the "line of fire." Pretending to be gay, they would infiltrate the inner circle of the Ladies of Newport. Or perhaps the volunteers were not pretending at all, as evidenced by the overall zealousness they put into their assignment. Since they could not be prosecuted during their mission, and since the findings had to leave no shadow of a doubt, the volunteers dove headfirst into their undercover mission. The undercover volunteers were instructed by the assistant secretary of the navy himself that the perpetrators must be caught in the act, and they were to follow their mission through to completion.

To make the method of evidence gathering even more bizarre, the volunteers kept elicit, detailed journals of their liaisons and meeting locations. One of the most popular gay pickup spots turned out to be one of modern-day Newport's most popular tourist attractions: Forty Steps on the Cliff Walk. With mounting pages of evidence, these handsome young navy decoys turned over their irrefutable findings to their superiors, who started making arrests—first among the navy personnel and then among the civilian population. The navy men were kept on board a prison ship; they were court-martialed, and some eventually did jail time. With Secretary Roosevelt's backing, the prosecution of the civilian population went full speed ahead as well, including the arrest of the well-respected Reverend Kent. It turns out that "lewd and scandalous behavior" (i.e. homosexuality) was a crime in 1919. It was characterized as a crime of perversion, and the civilians were prosecuted vigorously. This is the decision that turned an undercover sting operation into a public relations nightmare for the navy.

During the trial of the Reverend Kent, the navy's evidence-gathering techniques came to light. When the public discovered the navy's use of "under the covers" agents to infiltrate the gay population of Newport, there was a huge public outcry. The data-gathering procedure was considered worse than the "crimes of perversion" being committed. While there was unquestionable evidence that the reverend was repeatedly having sex with young sailors, he was acquitted because the proof of his sex crimes had been acquired using entrapment methods. There was even more of a public outcry when news surfaced that Assistant Secretary of the Navy Franklin D. Roosevelt had given the okay to the undercover operatives to proceed with vigor and use any and all means necessary to get to the bottom of these allegations.

In the short run, this Newport sex scandal might have cost FDR his shot at the vice presidency, as Republicans Warren Harding and Calvin Coolidge swamped him and his running mate, James Cox, at the ballot box in 1920. It seems like this scandal, like most shameful events, eventually faded from the limelight, and those involved moved on with their lives. FDR was eventually elected president and led our nation through two of its darkest moments: the Great Depression and World War II. Looking back at history, Franklin Roosevelt is considered one of this nation's greatest presidents and overall inspirational leaders. Throughout his life, Roosevelt continued to deny any knowledge of the interior mechanics of the operation to uncover the "wicked and immoral Ladies of Newport."

# LAY NAVY SCANDAL TO F. D. ROOSEVELT

## Senate Naval Sub-Committee Accuses Him and Daniels in Newport Inquiry.

## DETAILS ARE UNPRINTABLE

## Minority Report Asserts Charges of Immorally Employing Men Do Officials Injustice.

*Special to The New York Times.*

This headline shows the results of the official investigation of a gay sex scandal. Former secretary of state and future president Franklin D. Roosevelt was held partially responsible for employing straight sailors as undercover decoys. Like the headline says, "The Details Are Unprintable!" *Headline courtesy of the* New York Times.

A special Senate subcommittee was ordered to investigate the interrogation methods used to uncover the goings-on at the Newport Navy Base. In July 1921, the subcommittee revealed its findings, which were extremely harsh for former secretary of the navy Josephus Daniels and Assistant Secretary Roosevelt. Both were strongly denounced for their actions, and the committee stated that Daniels should have been court-martialed for "violating the code of the American citizen and ignoring the rights of every American boy who enlisted to fight for his country." As for chief machinist mate Ervin Arnold, the subcommittee recommended that his name should be forever stricken from the navy roster. Its findings went on to conclude that the actions of a handful of seamen in a group of over twenty thousand in no way demonstrate what the navy stands for. Essentially, it concluded that a rotten apple or two does not spoil the whole bushel. Newport, to this day, still has a strong naval presence and military heritage, which adds to the overall fabric of this diverse and colorful community.

# CHAPTER 11

# THE CURSED CAPTAIN

S hip crews and sea captains are, by nature, very superstitious. They are constantly watching the birds, the sky and even the sea itself for warnings or signs of impending doom. There have always been tall tales of some sailor who cursed the sea or acted in some way to anger the gods, only to bring doom and gloom to his ship or otherwise ruin the voyage. There was a captain from Rhode Island who must have done something horrifically against the laws of nature because he single-handedly participated in two of the worst maritime disasters in the Ocean State's history, including one just off the coast of Newport. His name was George McVey.

Captain McVey was in command of the 252-foot side-wheel paddle steamer *Larchmont*, which regularly sailed from Providence, Rhode Island, to New York City. February 11, 1907, would be no different, even though a winter gale was whipping waves up to twenty feet high and the temperature was approaching zero. This was of no concern to Captain McVey, a veteran seaman who had made this run dozens of times. Although the *Larchmont* was his first command, the twenty-seven-year-old captain made his normal preparations, and the steamer shoved off about 7:00 p.m., only thirty minutes behind schedule. Even though a winter storm was howling outside, Captain McVey was confident that this would be another routine voyage. At about 10:30 p.m., the steamer left the relatively calm confines of Narragansett Bay and headed southwest into Long Island Sound toward New York City. Captain McVey felt confident enough that, after checking the conditions in the pilothouse, he retired to his cabin and turned over the wheel to his first mate, John Anson.

Shortly thereafter, the bow watchman spotted two lights ahead, and Anson made the necessary adjustments, turning the *Larchmont* to another heading to avoid a collision. However, the approaching vessel, also seeking to avoid a collision, adjusted its course and was again steering directly into the *Larchmont*'s path. First Mate Anson hastily blew the ship's warning whistle and threw it hard to port, but the evasive maneuver came too late. The three-masted coal schooner *Harry Knowlton*, en route to Boston, came crashing down on the side of the *Larchmont*, almost instantly opening a gaping hole at the waterline and flooding the crippled passenger vessel. The frigid water killed many of the *Larchmont*'s passengers almost instantly, while the less fortunate would drown, trapped below deck. Many other passengers were killed or badly wounded by the ship's bursting steam pipes. The few unfortunate souls who made it above deck were quickly coated with water from the crashing waves and frozen almost in place. Captain McVey ordered the crew to ready the lifeboats and try to get the few remaining survivors off the sinking ship. By this time, the *Larchmont* had lost all power and was completely at the mercy of the churning sea. To make matters worse, the vessel that struck the *Larchmont*, the *Harry Knowlton*, sailed off, not knowing how much damage it had inflicted, and didn't bother to search for survivors or even alert authorities of the collision.

The first news of the wreck came at 6:09 a.m. on nearby Block Island, when a sixteen-year-old passenger washed up on the beach in front of the North Lighthouse mumbling, "More coming, more coming." Fishermen on the tiny island quickly sailed to the wreck site to see if any more survivors could be located. The brave rescuers would locate a deck section of the *Larchmont* with fifteen people onboard, eight alive and seven frozen to death. No more survivors among the more than two hundred passengers and crew would ever be found, although the captain and many of the crew men were later found floating in a lifeboat. During the inquiry of the sinking, Captain McVey had to fight charges of cowardice—abandoning his sinking ship to save himself while helpless passengers were left to fend for themselves in the dark, frigid night. The inquiry later determined that first mate John Anson's actions were insufficient in avoiding the collision. Unfortunately for Anson, he couldn't defend these charges because he, too, perished in the icy waters, while Captain McVey was exonerated in what would later be described as the "*Titanic* of New England."

But this wouldn't be the last time this captain would be involved in a maritime disaster. Eighteen years later, McVey was piloting a day steamer between Pawtucket and Newport, bringing summer revelers to enjoy the

The *Larchmont* was one of two vessels under the command of Captain George McVey that suffered terrible fates at sea. The side-wheeled steamer rammed another ship and sank in the icy waters just off the coast of Block Island, killing over two hundred passengers and earning the maritime disaster the nickname the *"Titanic* of New England." *Photo courtesy of Wikimedia commons.*

beachside resort before returning to the capital region in the evening. On August 18, 1925, after an uneventful day in Newport, the SS *Mackinaw* reloaded over six hundred passengers for the return trip to Pawtucket. These day-trippers had enjoyed a carefree day among the seaside charms of Newport, but their relaxing day was about to come to an abrupt end.

As the 152-foot steamer sailed north through Narragansett Bay, some of the passengers noticed a hissing sound coming from just below deck. Just as the steamer passed the Newport Navy Base, a massive explosion rocked the *Mackinaw*, scalding many of the passengers with boiling steam and causing many of those on deck to jump overboard to avoid the hot vapor and thick smoke. The *Mackinaw*'s boiler had exploded, but fortunately for the doomed ship and the unlucky Captain McVey, help was quick to arrive from the navy station. Dozens of boats arrived within minutes to ferry the injured passengers to the nearby Navy Hospital, as well as scoop up the terrified travelers who had jumped off the deck to avoid the inferno onboard the stricken steamer.

Sadly, fifty-five passengers would perish from their injuries sustained aboard the *Mackinaw*. But with over six hundred people sailing that afternoon, there is no question the explosion could have caused even more destruction. The proximity to the navy station, as well as the top-flight care given at the base hospital, certainly kept this tragedy to a minimum. Perhaps this was one of the few moments of good fortune Captain McVey would enjoy during his seafaring career. There is no denying that the cursed captain will forever be remembered for being part of two of Rhode Island's worst maritime disasters.

# CHAPTER 12

# THE STORM OF
# THE CENTURY

M any American cities have had watershed moments, where some
disaster, either natural or man-made, reshapes an area eternally.
The city of Chicago had a devastating fire in 1873; Galveston, Texas,
was nearly wiped off the map by a hurricane in 1900; and San Francisco
suffered a paralyzing earthquake in 1906. Each of these disasters irrevocably
altered these metropolitan areas' fortunes and left long-lasting physical and
psychological scars on the survivors for many generations to come. Newport,
and the state of Rhode Island, was no exception after experiencing the
"Storm of the Century": the 1938 hurricane.

Very few events have changed an area the way the Storm of the Century
did. What is even more amazing about the massive hurricane that wreaked
havoc on a vast portion of the northeastern United States is that it arrived
almost unannounced, taking the entire area by surprise, unprepared for such
a monstrous tempest. The National Weather Service (NWS) was certainly
aware of the massive and powerful hurricane's existence; it just sort of, for
lack of a better term, misplaced its location. On September 20, the NWS
issued a hurricane warning for Miami, Florida, yet the storm never made
landfall there, apparently curving northeast and heading harmlessly out
to sea. These were the days before radar and weather bureaus relied on
wind readings from oceangoing ships and measurements from land-based
barometers, essentially forecasting blind compared to the modern-day
technology used to track these killer storms. It is almost hard to believe that
a five-hundred-mile-wide hurricane, which at one point was a Category

5, could hit a major population center like the Northeast corridor of the United States virtually undetected. Yet on September 21, 1938, fantasy became reality as the Storm of the Century unleashed its fury on, first, eastern Long Island and then New England, slamming Rhode Island with previously unseen and unimaginable ferocity.

The first landmass to feel the brunt of the killer storm was eastern Long Island, which was experiencing more than one-hundred-mile-per-hour winds just after 2:00 p.m. The hurricane was moving at an incredible northward speed at this point, an almost unheard-of seventy miles per hour. This rare and rapid northward speed prevented the Northeast's best defense mechanism against monster tropical storms from actually taking place. Usually when a hurricane hits the icy waters of the North Atlantic, cold water is sucked into the storm's internal engine, sapping its power supply—warm tropical water—and the storm loses its intensity. Cold water is usually the Northeast's last line of defense. However, in this case, the storm moved so rapidly that the monster had no time to die. It was on a mission to destroy, and its next stop was the Rhode Island coast, waiting unprotected just to the north.

By 3:00 p.m., little Block Island felt the storm's intensity, with thirty-five out of fifty boats of the island's fishing fleet destroyed. The southern coast of Rhode Island was next, with more than 120-mile-per-hour winds smashing the coastline and pulverizing entire beachfront communities with twenty-plus-foot storm surges, drowning the inhabitants who survived the first wave of the attack. The community of Napatree point in Watch Hill, Rhode Island, was especially hard hit. Before the storm, this sliver of sandy beach held thirty-nine oceanfront houses that had stood up to gales for many years. This storm was different, and the tiny peninsula was no match for the howling winds and raging sea. Everything would be entirely lost here; the thirty-nine houses were almost instantly splintered and washed completely away, and only fifteen of the forty-two residents of the tony beach community would survive. Many survivors clung for hours to the shattered, floating remains of their beach homes. The beach was utterly washed clean of any trace of human existence.

Most of the southern coast of Rhode Island was treated in the same violent fashion. Charlestown Beach was also wiped clean as if a giant eraser had been swept over the area. Narragansett's famous Dunes Club was also destroyed, and the sea wall, which was supposed to protect the area, was pummeled as well. Needles to say, many break walls and sea walls built to contain and minimize damage and flooding failed miserably. Mother Nature

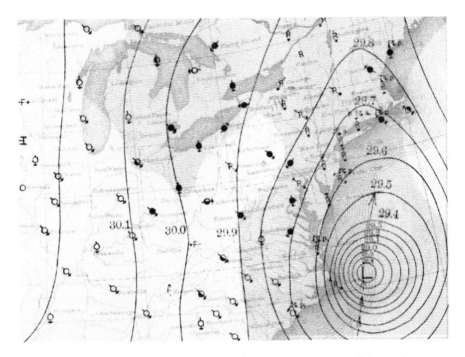

This map shows the path of the infamous 1938 hurricane on its course of destruction toward the Rhode Island coast. Forecasters gave local residents no warning of the killer storm's arrival, and when the hurricane landed unexpectedly, it was too late to evacuate. *Map courtesy of the National Weather Service.*

was certainly no match for the constraints man tried to implement to contain her wrath; she easily brushed them aside with her seemingly unlimited power and force.

The storm now turned its attention northward to the Island of Jamestown, sitting helplessly in Narragansett Bay. This small island would experience a tragedy so horrific that it still resonates in the community today. Norman Caswell was driving a handful of schoolchildren home on that fateful afternoon, like he did every day. The day had started out like many late September days—fairly mild, a little overcast and a bit breezy—but that morning, there were no serious indications of the powerful storm that was headed this way. By late afternoon, heavy winds and rain had started to buffet the island. Norman Caswell loaded his eight passengers from Thomas Clarke Elementary School and started the fateful journey. The kids on his bus all lived on the southern tip of Jamestown, which meant the bus had to cross a narrow strip of beach at Mackerel Cove. The area is a public beach and connects the southern tip of the island by a small sandy strip. It is essentially at sea level. To make matters worse, the tide was at its peak for the day, compounding the effect of the rising wind and storm surge.

As the bus started across the narrow strip of road, the water was already up to the tires, but Caswell pushed forward. By this time, the winds had reached one hundred miles an hour, and rain was pelting the metal exterior ferociously. The children on board must have been terrified, yet Caswell pressed on, inching his way across the swollen passage. About halfway across, the bus stalled, with the engine becoming flooded by the rapidly rising surf. All efforts to restart the bus failed, and Caswell reasoned that his best chance to save the children was to form a human chain and forge their way to the west side of the beach, where four of the children lived on Fox Hill Farm. The farm, less than a quarter mile away, would be a simple stroll on any other day. But on September 21, 1938, the simple stroll turned into "the march from hell." Joe Matoes, who lived on the farm and had four kids on the bus, watched from the west side of the causeway as the faint outlines of nine bodies, arm in arm, slowly trudged toward the farm's higher ground. Sadly, they would never make it; a powerful wave crashed over the beach and washed the helpless schoolchildren away, right in front of one horrified father. The four Matoes children, as well as Constantine and John Giantis and Marion Chellis, all became victims of the killer storm. Norman Caswell survived the massive wave, as did eleven-year-old Clayton Chellis, son of the Beavertail Light keeper. Chellis was an excellent swimmer and survived by floating on the monster wave, finally washing ashore almost three miles north where the foot of the Jamestown Bridge stands today.

Although an excellent swimmer, poor Clayton Chellis was doomed to drown. He was skating in Jamestown a couple years later when he fell through the ice but was pulled to safety. When he was eighteen, Chellis joined the navy to fight for his country and survived to the war's end. In 1946, he was celebrating his orders to return to the States when he went swimming to explore some reefs off the Island of Saipan in the South Pacific. Perhaps it was too much drinking or a deadly undertow, but the sea finally claimed Clayton Chellis at the age of nineteen, eight years after he survived that terrible storm back home.

Norman Caswell would always be vilified on Jamestown after his fateful decision to take the kids off the bus. He told anyone who would listen that he thought they would be "drowned like rats" if they stayed onboard and figured a human chain would be their best chance at returning home safely. As it turned out, Caswell's decision went horribly wrong, and he died a few short years later from depression and alcohol consumption.

The seven children weren't the only victims in the area. A few miles from Jamestown Island, keeper Walter Eberly lost his life when Whale Rock Lighthouse was swept off its base and into the raging waves. His body was never found, and the lighthouse would never be rebuilt. The wave size that carried the lighthouse off its foundation was estimated at over twenty feet. Many things in Newport, and the rest of New England, would never be the same. Residents who survived through the night could do little—just hunker down and hold on tight until morning. Just seven hours later, the storm was over, and sunrise revealed a new landscape. The light of the new day revealed a swath of devastation that would take over a generation to repair.

The damage from the 1938 hurricane could be measured in dollars—over $4 billion in today's economy—but the larger damage might have come to people's psyches. Many people would be changed forever. Jamestown quickly constructed a bridge to the mainland to allow a faster escape route in case another killer storm came its way. Ferry service was just too dangerous during violent storms and eventually would be phased out. Train service between New York and Boston was disrupted for months, and people turned to a new mode of transportation—airline travel—and never looked back. Entire beach communities had been wiped off the map, never to be rebuilt. Beaches and dunes that had taken hundreds of years to form were erased overnight. Every nautical chart was rendered useless overnight as well; the hurricane created new inlets and channels and closed others in the blink of an eye, causing the rewriting of centuries-old sailing maps. The city of Providence, which endured thirteen-foot-high floodwaters in the downtown area, constructed massive hurricane gates at the southern edge of the city that can be closed if a monster wall of water heads its way again. The damage to property was enormous, with over fifty-seven thousand buildings destroyed or severely damaged, as well as over 2,500 boats wrecked. The loss of life was high too; 682 people perished in the storm, with over 100 in Rhode Island alone, mostly from drowning or being hit by falling trees. Twenty-six thousand cars were smashed, 275 million trees were uprooted, 1,600 livestock died and an estimated 750,000 chickens were killed during the storm. The hurricane wasn't selective; it was equally destructive to man and beast. There were still trees being cleared that had fallen during the storm in remote sections of New England into the 1950s. The devastation was astounding and widespread. There were wind speeds measuring as high at 186 miles per hour, strong enough to peel paint off cars. Newport weathered the storm as well as could be hoped. The beaches and Ocean Drive bore the brunt of the assault and were decimated. Sections of the famed Ocean Drive were

The power of the 1938 hurricane is evident from this photo. A Boston-bound train is literally stuck in its tracks, blocked by storm debris and even a small fishing boat. Scenes like this were repeated throughout New England. *Photo courtesy of Wikimedia commons.*

washed into the raging sea, and the beach pavilion at super exclusive Bailey's Beach was smashed, except for a small section that was gently placed at the center of the street out front.

The mansions on Bellevue Avenue survived remarkably well thanks to their high perch above the sea and their sturdy stone construction. Parts of the cliff walk were not so lucky, however, with walkways along the southern section overturned and stone walls along the side of the trail violently uprooted. The damage was so extensive that it has still not been repaired to this day. The same can be said for the Easton's Beach amusement park—a wildly popular summer getaway. The large beachfront park included a giant roller coaster, a merry-go-round and a monster Ferris wheel, as well as a long boardwalk running the length of the beach. On the morning of September 22, it was all gone, crushed to pieces, as if a giant, ill-tempered child had grown tired of his play toy and smashed it apart with one violent thrust of his hand. The Easton's Beach amusement park would never be rebuilt—another relic of Newport summers gone forever, living on only in people's memories.

Survivors did what they could to pick up the pieces of their shattered homes and lives. The dead who were recovered were buried; homes that could be salvaged were repaired. Those structures that were beyond repair were torn down or burned to make way for something new to take their place. The business of life slowed returned to normal as best it could. The area and the nation were still in the grip of the Great Depression, and money and jobs were tight. This was a difficult time for the region as a whole. Recovering

Newport's Easton's Beach was famous for its large amusement park, which included a Ferris wheel, roller coaster and Olympic-sized swimming pool. On September 21, 1938, a powerful and unanticipated hurricane washed it away without a trace. *Photo courtesy of the author.*

from a massive storm was hard enough, but the drumbeat of war in Europe and Japan was on the horizon. Without question, it was a time of great sacrifice and uncertainty. People persevered, and things would eventually return to normal. Still, many people's perceptions of the sea were altered forever. There is no question that people who lived through this horrific tempest kept a wary eye on the water, always on the lookout for the next "Storm of the Century."

# CHAPTER 13

# SCANDALS AND SECRETS ON THE HIGH SEAS

There seems to be a public perception that Newport has always hosted (and still does) the most famous race in yachting: the America's Cup. However, this is not true. The first race wasn't called the America's Cup; it wasn't even held in the United States. The first match race was held off the Isle of Wight in 1851 and was called the 100 Guinea Cup, in reference to a no-longer-used form of British currency. The Royal Yacht Squadron, which was hosting the race, preferred the term the "Queen's Cup" in honor of Her Majesty, Queen Victoria. So in 1851, the commodore of the newly formed New York Yacht Club sent a schooner christened the *America* to challenge fifteen British yachts on a fifty-three-mile regatta around the Isle of Wight. It was only then, after the *America*'s resounding victory, that the cup was named in honor of the winning vessel.

Queen Victoria was present at the finish line for the race and asked naïvely, "Who came in second?" The response was rather prophetic: "Your Majesty, there is no second!" However, there was controversy over this first race. Many British teams insisted that the *America* won only because it did not round all the marks on the racecourse. These rumors were never proven. The New York Yacht Club took its winning trophy home to the Big Apple, and in its hands it would stay for the next 132 years.

As holder of the America's Cup, the New York Yacht Club (NYYC) was able to select the venue for the races and also the size and design of the yachts competing. The new rules also stipulated that the challengers must tell the champion not only the size of the boat they were planning to enter but

The "Auld Mug" is the trophy given to the victorious team in the America's Cup yacht race. Some of the world's richest men and largest egos have spent their lives and vast fortunes just to say, "I own the cup!" *Photo courtesy of the author.*

also the riggings and sails being used. This allowed the Americans to know exactly what the enemy was planning ahead of time and how to counteract the challenge. The first challenge races were actually held off the coast of New Jersey at Sandy Hook.

There is no question the NYYC did everything in its power to ensure the cup—or the "Auld Mug," as it was now called—remained in American hands. One such rule it instituted was that all competing boats must sail to the venue, which meant yacht crews must endure a treacherous and grueling Atlantic crossing, even before vying for control of the cup. Many British syndicates spent millions of dollars and thousands of hours trying to design a boat fast enough to defeat the champions, all for the honor and privilege of hoisting a three-foot-high silver trophy. The expression "Britannia rules the waves but America waves the rules" was a popular refrain amongst the opposing yachts for many years to come.

In 1895, Lord Dunraven of Scotland mounted a challenge to retake the cup back to the United Kingdom with his innovatively designed schooner *Valkyrie III*. Lord Dunraven was sure his new design would be up to the task with a stronger steel mast and hull, instead of a less durable wooden design, and a wider base along the waterline. But Dunraven's new design was no match for the Herreshoff-designed *Defender*, which easily bested the opponent. Nathanael Herreshoff was from nearby Bristol, Rhode Island, and was considered the preeminent yacht designer in the world. His cutting-edge designs used new, stronger and lighter materials like aluminum and featured more aerodynamic hulls. Herreshoff had his cutting-edge design built in a closed-off hanger and launched at night so as to conceal its construction. The *Defender* also used aluminum topside riveted to steel frames and manganese bronze below waters. *Valkyrie III* lost the first race and then was unceremoniously disqualified in the second race following a collision with the *Defender* before the starting line, despite finishing first, and in turn withdrew from the contest. Dunraven also complained that there were too many spectator boats crowding the racecourse and hindering his boat.

The disqualification left Dunraven in a bitter disagreement with all parties over the fairness of the race committee's impartiality. He was sure the NYYC had cheated to ensure that its boat would reclaim the prize. This controversy put an end to Lord Dunraven's yachting career. His honorary New York Yacht Club membership was revoked, and he was sure no contending boat would ever receive a fair shake against the home team. Lord Dunraven's accusations left many observers wondering if the America's Cup races would continue, or would this controversy put an end to the yacht races forever?

Despite the contentious and strained feelings over the 1895 America's Cup controversy, a new contender stepped up in 1899 and took up the chase for the honor of hoisting the cup. Sir Thomas Lipton of the famed tea company would be the next challenger for the prestigious trophy, but the Herreshoff-designed American yacht *Columbia* again proved too fast for the challenger, *Shamrock*. Sir Thomas Lipton would unsuccessfully vie for the America's Cup four more times but would be repelled every time. His last challenge for the prestigious trophy was in 1930, when the race venue was moved from Sandy Hook, New Jersey, to Newport, Rhode Island. Lipton spent over $1 million on a new yacht, and despite the stock market crash, the cup challenge went on as scheduled. Lipton's outclassed wooden *Shamrock V* was easily bested by the sleek J-boat *Enterprise*, with Harold Stirling Vanderbilt of the Marble House at the helm. Lipton died in 1931, heartbroken that he never tasted victory in the world's most prestigious yacht race.

In 1934, British aviation designer and industrialist Sir Thomas Sopwith was next in line to challenge for the silver mug. Sopwith's innovative steel-plated design of his entry, the *Endeavor*, made him the favorite against Harold Vanderbilt's defender, *Rainbow*. Sopwith's *Endeavor* actually won the first two races, and it looked like the New York Yacht Club's winning streak might finally be coming to an end. But a dispute in pay caused the *Endeavor*'s original crew to strike, and Sopwith was forced to sail with amateurs. Poor racing tactics and the inexperience of the amateur crew finally caught up with the faster *Endeavor*, and the *Rainbow* cruised to easy wins in the next four races and retained the cup. Once again, the home team had dodged a bullet thanks to Sopwith's frugality, and the winning streak continued. Harold Vanderbilt would easily win his third America's Cup in 1937 with his self-financed schooner *Ranger*, which was extremely high tech for its day. The *Ranger* was the first yacht to be largely constructed of a new lightweight yet sturdy material called aluminum. After 1937, the America's Cup challenges went on a long hiatus because of World War II and the extreme expense of the large J-class yachts used in the races.

In 1956, the New York Yacht Club, in an attempt to restore interest in the cup match races, decided to switch the class of boat that could vie for the coveted trophy. The more economical twelve-meter class was chosen, and any boat whose length, girth and sail area was equal to or less than twelve meters was eligible to compete. Many innovative and controversial designs would ensue over the next few decades with the adoption of this new class of yachts eligible to race. The new twelve-meter class also opened up the race to colorful and boisterous yacht owners and designers from other countries around the world. The 1977 America's Cup was defended by the self-proclaimed "Mouth of the South," Ted Turner, as captain of an all-aluminum twelve-meter called *Courageous*. Although Turner defended the cup successfully, he did not win many friends among the racing fraternity in Newport. His loud and drunken behavior even got him banned from the yachter's favorite watering hole in Newport, the Black Pearl. The boat Turner defeated in 1977 was from Australia, and its flamboyant and controversial owner, Alan Bond, swore he would be back and that the cup would be returning with him to Australia.

In 1983, Alan Bond was back, and this time he had a secret weapon with him. His yacht, the *Australia II*, had a newly designed and controversial winged keel that would make it easier to turn—and theoretically faster than the competition. The design was so controversial that the New York Yacht Club filed a lawsuit to keep the boat with from competing. The lawsuit was disallowed, and racing would commence. The Australian team was super secretive about its innovative keel design, so much so that it covered it with a green tarp while not racing to shield the top-secret configuration from prying eyes. One morning, at about 2:00 a.m., the *Australia II* security personnel noticed bubbles coming up from under the yacht. After shining searchlights on the water and under the boat, they discovered a frogman swimming beneath the keel trying to photograph or vandalize the hull. Actually, no one is quite sure of the frogman's intent; he slipped away into the harbor and was never apprehended. This was another sign to Alan Bond that the New York Yacht Club would do whatever it took to "Win at all Costs!"

This is the winged keel of the 1983 America's Cup–winning yacht *Australia II*. This secret weapon was the difference, enabling the Australians to break the Americans' 132-year winning streak. *Photo courtesy of Wikimedia commons.*

The American entry, *Liberty*, and its captain, Dennis Connor, actually had a 2–0 lead, but *Australia II* and its innovative design would win four of the next five races, including the decisive final matchup, to finally wrestle the America's Cup from the greedy hands of the New York Yacht Club.

On September 26, 1983, the longest winning streak in sports history, 132 years, finally came to an end. The NYYC filed one final appeal, claiming the Dutch actually came up with the innovative design used by the Aussies. If this claim could be proven, the *Australia II* would be forced to forfeit the cup for violating the rule that different countries could not share and collaborate on conceptual design ideas. An investigation determined there was no merit to the claim, and the trophy was transferred to the Royal Perth Yacht Club, the new owner of the America's Cup.

There was mass hysteria among the Australian supporters in Newport and worldwide when the Aussies finally hoisted the cup. The city of Newport and the world yachting community were in shock, and many wondered how 132 years of victory, with the last 53 years of races taking place in Newport, had finally come to an end. The majority of the blame

The *Defender*, owned by prominent Newporter William K. Vanderbilt, was a classic J-boat used in the 1895 America's Cup yacht races. *Defender* was the first all-metal and aluminum-designed yacht raced in the America's Cup and was considered cutting edge for its day. *Photo courtesy of Wikimedia commons.*

was directed at one man, *Liberty* captain Dennis Connor. There were rumors that the *Liberty*'s crew was complacent and outright disrespected the upstart *Australia II*'s chances for victory. This might have led to an overconfidence that certainly backfired when the underdog yacht with the mysterious winged keel carried the cup back home to the Land Down Under. *Australia II* owner Alan Bond was as boisterous and flamboyant as ever, immediately hoisting the winning twelve-meter out of the water at Bannister's Wharf for the entire world to see. But by revealing the secret keel, the genie was out of the bottle, and the boating world raced to copy the configuration of the winning America's Cup boat.

Australia's America's Cup winning streak was short lived, and it promptly lost the 1987 defense to disgraced captain Dennis Connor, who redeemed himself to some degree by recouping the trophy. Since Connor was sailing for the San Diego Yacht Club, the cup defenses would be held on the West Coast and are likely never to return to the City by the Sea, thus ending Newport's undisputed reign as the "Sailing Capital

The *Oracle* is a cutting-edge catamaran now used in the America's Cup yacht races. As you can see, as technology has advanced, so has the design of these super-fast and sleek watercrafts. *Photo courtesy of Wikimedia commons.*

of the World." The current cup holder is American racing team *Oracle*, owned by Oracle Software founder Larry Ellison. Ellison has spent millions of dollars reclaiming the America's Cup and bringing it back to our shores. One thing is certain, the "Auld Mug" will be fought over for years to come by multibillionaires with seemingly endless bank rolls who will spare no expense for the privilege and right to say, "I own the America's Cup."

# CHAPTER 14

# CAMELOT, NEWPORT STYLE

Camelot was the mythical castle of King Arthur and his Knights of the Round Table, where everyone lived in perfect harmony and idyllic happiness. Camelot was also the slogan given to John F. Kennedy's presidency by his wife, former Newport debutante Jacqueline Bouvier. Jackie thought the young and vibrantly charismatic president would bring new hope and optimism to the country at the start of the 1960s. But as we all know, fairy tales don't always have happy endings. When we peel back the curtain and examine this version of Camelot a little more closely, we will see it wasn't much of an enchanted fantasy after all. This narrative was more of a public relations creation, expertly woven by a maniacal family patriarch, Joseph P. Kennedy Sr., than a place of peace, hope and harmony.

Joe Kennedy Sr. was born into a prominent and influential East Boston family and learned at an early age how political connections and influential friends were the keys to a successful and lucrative future. He demonstrated this skill when he chose Rose Fitzgerald to be his bride in 1914. Rose Fitzgerald's father was former Democratic congressman and Boston mayor John "Honey Fitz" Fitzgerald, a man of seemingly limitless political connections. Many of these political connections would open private doors to Joe Kennedy Sr. in the worlds of politics and high finance. Through many of these prominent connections, Joe Kennedy Sr. would amass a sizable fortune via stock market manipulation, insider trading and bootlegging liquor during Prohibition. Because of Kennedy's well-placed friends, he was able to purchase the rights to distribute Gordon's Gin and

Dewar's Scotch in America just before Prohibition was rescinded. Kennedy had inside information that the Eighteenth Amendment would be repealed, and because of his inside knowledge, he was poised to capitalize in a big way.

Joe Kennedy Sr. also made large investments in the fledgling movie industry, just in its infancy in Hollywood. Kennedy was ruthless in his business dealings and would do whatever was necessary to get his way. Kennedy and his group of investors were purchasing small movie studios throughout the 1920s and eventually merged them all into the powerful RKO studio group, one of the largest and most powerful entities in Hollywood. As chief of this powerful studio, Joe Kennedy also had access to a bevy of young actresses and starlets at his disposal and certainly took full advantage of the situation. Kennedy would constantly help himself to his endless supply of young ladies, willing to do anything to make it big in the movies. One of Joe Kennedy's most famous conquests was an up-and-coming actress named Gloria Swanson, who had successfully made the transition from silent films to talkies and would later star in one of Hollywood's most enduring films, *Sunset Boulevard*. Also during this time, Kennedy was attempting to buy out the successful Pantages Theatre chain, but owner Alexander Pantages spurned the $8 million offer Kennedy made. Pantages would soon discover how ruthless Joe Kennedy could be when it came to negotiating. In 1929, during the meltdown on Wall Street, Alexander Pantages was arrested and charged with the rape of a seventeen-year-old would-be vaudeville dancer named Eunice Pringle. Pringle alleged that Pantages had attacked her in a tiny side office of his downtown theater after inviting her in to audition. Pantages was tried, convicted and sentenced to fifty years in prison, despite his claims that he was "SET UP." Pantages triumphed in the second trial by theatrically demonstrating how impractical a rape was inside his broom closet and planting in the jurors' minds the suggestion that Eunice Pringle might have been paid by business rivals, especially Kennedy. But the damage had been done to the theater owner's reputation, and Kennedy and his investors were able to capitalize and purchase the movie houses for a bargain price of $3.5 million.

Joe Kennedy demonstrated that he would use any means necessary to acquire what he desired, and his aspirations would eventually lead all the way to the presidency and the White House. This would also be a trait he would instill in his young family, the same family he had neglected and been unfaithful to while gallivanting around Hollywood with young starlets. This would be a fable he would perpetuate throughout his life—masquerading as a loving husband while his devoted wife, Rose, raised the growing clan.

Kennedy would cuddle up to his family only when a photo opportunity or positive media story presented itself. The patriarch was a master at using the media to portray himself as a great family man and tout the accomplishments of his gifted family. Womanizing and neglecting one's family were two characteristics the elder Kennedy would pass on to his sons, all of whom were eager to carry on the family tradition.

After Joe Kennedy reaped his ill-gotten profits by capitalizing on the demise of Wall Street, the repeal of Prohibition and the exploitation of Hollywood, the business tycoon turned his attention to politics. Kennedy had donated large sums of money to the Franklin D. Roosevelt election campaign with the hopes of securing a cabinet seat inside the new administration. Roosevelt had other ideas for Kennedy in his administration, appointing him director of the newly created Securities and Exchange Commission. Kennedy's position would require him to clean up the illegal practices like insider trading and stock manipulation on Wall Street. Ironically, Kennedy had immensely profited from these very practices he was now in charge of eliminating. Roosevelt's thought process was evident when he commented on the new SEC chairman's appointment and his role in cleaning up the securities industry Kennedy had pilfered only years earlier: "It takes a crook to catch a crook." Roosevelt knew that no one had more insider knowledge of how Wall Street's illegal and contemptible practices were carried out, and he sought to level the playing field for all investors.

As a reward for his service in creating the Securities and Exchange Commission, Joseph P. Kennedy Sr. was appointed ambassador to the court of Saint James, in London, England, in 1938. This was a perfect opportunity for Kennedy and his family to mingle with London's high society and royalty, despite the growing threat of war in Europe. Kennedy was considered an appeaser and even tried to set up meetings with Adolph Hitler to work out the differences between Germany and the United States. This was in sharp contrast to the recommendations of Parliament member Winston Churchill, who wanted Hitler stopped at all costs. Kennedy also argued strongly against giving military and economic aid to the United Kingdom.

Kennedy committed political suicide when he stated that "Democracy was dead in England" and still wanted a negotiated settlement with Hitler, even after the Nazis had bombed London. It had become clear to the Roosevelt administration that Kennedy was attempting to further his political career and did not have the best interest of his country at heart. By this time, it had become apparent that the policy of appeasing Hitler and trying to negotiate with this maniacal dictator would not work. Hitler was focused on world domination, and Kennedy had badly underestimated the outcome: a pending world war. When it was clear that Kennedy had wrongly backed diplomacy, the outcry from the American public was too loud to ignore, and the ambassador was asked to resign. Any aspirations Joseph Kennedy Sr. harbored of ever becoming president were now gone, and he quietly exited public life. Kennedy's political career would now be focused on his sons, whom he would attempt to mold into viable candidates while acting as their puppet master, pulling all the right strings to get them into elected offices.

Joe's best hope for a presidential candidate was his oldest son, Joseph Kennedy Jr. Joe Jr. was an intelligent and handsome Harvard-educated young man who was very popular with his fellow students. At the outbreak of World War II, the young Kennedy left Harvard Law School a year early to enlist in the U.S. Navy as a bomber pilot. After successfully completing twenty-five missions flying antisubmarine patrols, Joe Kennedy Jr. was eligible to return stateside but felt it was his duty to continue fighting the Germans. He volunteered for a secret mission, where planes would be fully loaded with powerful explosives. The pilots would bail out, and the flying bombs would be radio controlled to destroy the targets. Kennedy was chosen to be the pilot for the first mission, and with twenty-one thousand pounds of high explosives in his B-24 bomber, he took off from England on July 23, 1944, to destroy a German weapons plant in France. Kennedy was to manually arm the bomb and then parachute out of the plane, while another aircraft in pursuit would remotely control the flying explosives into the munitions plant. After manually arming the weapon, the pilot and copilot would have ten minutes to safely exit the plane, but something went terribly wrong. Just two minutes after arming the bomb, the high explosives prematurely detonated and pulverized the aircraft over the coast of southwest England. Kennedy and his copilot were killed instantly, as were the hopes of Joseph Kennedy Sr. ever getting his namesake elected to be president of the United States.

The distraught father would now turn his political ambitions toward his next-oldest son. The frail and often sickly John Fitzgerald Kennedy would be a long shot to ever hold the highest office in the land, but if anyone could pull it off, Joe Kennedy Sr. could. He had the deep pockets, political connections and media public relations spin machine to make it possible. He just needed to create a war hero to start his political machine in motion, and he pulled every string in his arsenal to make it happen for his son John.

With an outpouring of nationalism and patriotism, many young men of John Kennedy's era left college to enlist in the military and seek revenge for the Japanese surprise attack on Pearl Harbor. JFK's grand plan would encounter one major roadblock along the way, however; he was rejected for army service because he failed the physical. Joe Kennedy Sr. stepped in and arranged a position for his son with the Office of Naval Intelligence, which eventually led to an appointment to the Motor Torpedo Boat Squadron Training Center in Melville, Rhode Island. The only way JFK could have received such an appointment with his chronic bad back was through the extensive political connections of his well-placed father. After training, and a short stint in Panama, it was off to the South Pacific and war against the Japanese for Lieutenant Kennedy as commander of *PT-109*.

On August 2, 1943, Lieutenant Kennedy's *PT-109*, as well as fourteen other patrol boats, were taking part in nighttime operations, attempting to disrupt the resupply of Japanese soldiers in the Solomon Islands. Kennedy's boat was idling silently, with only one engine running to avoid detection, observing enemy troop movements close by, when one of the American crew men noticed a large ship about to hit them. A Japanese destroyer was barreling toward Kennedy and his boat, and with less than ten seconds to react, there was nothing the novice commander could do. The destroyer split *PT-109* in half, killing two sailors instantly and severely wounding two others. Lieutenant Kennedy would also reinjure his chronic bad back, but

Captain John F. Kennedy and his crew of *PT-109*, which would eventually be sunk when it was rammed by a Japanese destroyer during a skirmish in the South Pacific. His story of survival and heroism would help to launch his political career. *Photo courtesy of U.S. Navy Archives.*

this did not prevent him from swimming to a nearby island with a badly burned crew man in tow. Once the injured men were safely secured on the island, Lieutenant Kennedy swam nearly four more miles to enlist the help of friendly natives, who carried a message inscribed inside a coconut to Allied patrols in the area. Kennedy and his men were finally rescued six days later, subsisting solely on coconuts. The *PT-109* crew's rescue was considered a miracle. After reports of the boat's collision and explosion, the navy actually held a memorial service for the sailors, never expecting to find any of them alive in the heavily patrolled Japanese-controlled waters. Kennedy was awarded the Navy and Marine Corps Medal for his lifesaving actions following the collision, although later in life he privately admitted to friends he didn't feel he deserved the medals he had received because the *PT-109* sinking had been the result of a botched military operation that had cost the lives of two members of his crew. When asked by interviewers how he became a war hero, Kennedy's candid reply was: "It was involuntary. They sank my boat."

Joe Kennedy Sr. now had his war hero to prop up into public office, and the public relations machine was revved up to full speed for John Kennedy's new career in politics. JFK's first elected political office was representing the largely Democratic section of east Boston in the House of Representatives from 1947 to 1952. It was during this stint as congressman that John Kennedy's connection to Newport, Rhode Island, began. During a dinner party in 1952, the newly elected Senator Kennedy met former debutante of the year and photographer for the *Washington Times Herald* Jacqueline Bouvier. Jackie's mother, Janet, had previously divorced notorious womanizer and gambler "Black Jack" Bouvier in favor of the more stable and much wealthier Hugh Auchincloss. Auchincloss was a successful New York stock broker whose family were original stock holders in John D. Rockefeller's Standard Oil Company. Auchincloss also came with a Fifth Avenue apartment and a Newport estate called Hammersmith Farm and was considered the largest collector of pornography in the world.

After JFK and Jackie announced their engagement, Newport's Saint Mary's Church was chosen as the location for the wedding, which took place on September 12, 1953. Almost 700 people packed into the church for the ceremony, and over 1,200 guests attended the reception at the family's three-hundred-acre waterfront estate to congratulate the newly married couple. One person who was not in attendance was Jackie's father. He was banned from the ceremony when Jackie's mom was alerted that Black Jack's night of heavy drinking had continued well into the wedding day. Janet decided that

Then senator John F. Kennedy and his new bride, Jacqueline, are seen sharing a private moment together after their wedding ceremony in Newport on September 12, 1953. It is unlikely that at this peaceful moment the young couple ever could have imagined how tumultuous and tragic their lives would become over the next ten years. *Photo courtesy of the Toni Frissell collection.*

sober stepfather Hugh Auchincloss was a much better choice to walk Jackie down the aisle than a still-intoxicated Jack Bouvier. John Kennedy chose his brother Robert and Florida senator George Smathers to be his co–best men, and his brother Edward was an usher. The happy couple would honeymoon in Acapulco, Mexico, and then return to California to visit old friend and future brother in-law Hollywood actor Peter Lawford. John had asked Jackie to return to Washington, D.C., without him, as he wanted to spend some time on the West Coast with old pal Lawford, but Jackie knew what her new husband really wanted: time away from his new wife to quench his seemingly endless lust for women. Jackie had wrongly assumed JFK's vows would end his days of womanizing, but she was sorely mistaken. Jackie refused to return to D.C. alone, preferring instead to keep an eye on her wandering husband. But it would be only a matter of time until Kennedy continued his decadent ways, just like his father had a generation earlier.

Now that John Kennedy had the appearance of the perfect family, with a former debutante as his wife and children on the way, he and his personal-handler father could now turn their attention to the ultimate prize: the presidency of the United States. The Kennedy team targeted the 1960 election and once again would do whatever it took to get its way. Kennedy would win the 1960 election over Republican candidate Richard Nixon by the narrowest margin in presidential history. One thing that swayed the opinion of many of the voters was the first televised debate against incumbent vice president Richard Nixon. Kennedy appeared youthful and vibrant and had a healthy glow on the nation's black-and-white TV sets. Nixon, on the other hand, appeared nervous, sweaty and sinister with the lack of makeup on his stubbly face. Over eighty million people watched this media first, and many undecided voters felt obligated to vote for the tan, confident presidential contender solely based on his good looks.

The Kennedys also used some old friends in Chicago to ensure the election turned out in their favor. Chicago mayor Richard Daley Jr. may have tampered with the actual vote count within the city, and mafia boss Sam Giancana reportedly influenced the vote as well. Giancana, who was extremely influential with area union members, may have persuaded many voters to cast their ballots for Kennedy with cash payments and other favors. Giancana was reportedly assisting the campaign as a favor to a former bootlegger from the old days, Joe Kennedy. Giancana reasoned that if he could help to get Kennedy elected, the new president would certainly be grateful and return the favor in a big way. Unfortunately, the powerful mob boss would feel double crossed when John appointed his brother Bobby as attorney general. Bobby's first order of business as the nation's top lawyer was to crack down on organized crime and the mafia chief himself.

Joe Kennedy Sr. finally felt vindicated; the conniving, backstabbing businessman finally bought his son the White House. And now that John Kennedy was president, would he finally outgrow his adolescent behavior, honor his marriage vows and actually be the family man he publically pretended to be? The honest and frank answer was a resounding no. Now that Kennedy was the most powerful man in the world, he would take his womanizing and philandering to an almost unimaginable level. Over the next few years, Kennedy would sleep with an astonishing number of women, many times carrying on these brazen acts of infidelity right under his wife's nose.

The most famous of Kennedy's seemingly never-ending list of mistresses was Marilyn Monroe, one of Hollywood's most famous and desirable actresses. Kennedy was introduced to the starlet by brother-in-law Peter Lawford, who was hosting a dinner party to honor the president in February 1962. The chemistry between the couple was instantly visible to all those in attendance. The president invited Marilyn to visit him in March on an upcoming trip to Palm Springs, California, where he would be staying at the estate of actor Bing Crosby. The couple was hanging out at the pool relaxing, and Marilyn became extremely intoxicated. However, there was no question to those at the compound that the couple was intimate, and Marilyn spent the night with the president. This tryst would eventually have tragic consequences for Marilyn; she would become obsessed with the charismatic president, while Kennedy on the other hand regarded the blond bombshell as another impressive notch on his ever-expanding bedpost. JFK even made a comment to Marilyn that she wasn't first-wife material, trying to let her down as easily as possible. Monroe was delusional that Kennedy would divorce his wife to marry her, but this would never occur. Despite her frequent calls to the White House, John Kennedy was done with her.

Apparently, the fact that Kennedy wasn't returning her calls was driving her crazy and only increased her drug use. John dispatched his brother Attorney General Robert Kennedy to California to deal with the obsessed Marilyn. Apparently, Marilyn was talking to anyone who would listen about her affair with the disinterested president, and Bobby's job was to shut her up. Speculation had run wild that Bobby, John and Frank Sinatra were all having simultaneous affairs with Marilyn and that she had threatened to hold a press conference exposing all the intimate details of the long-running affairs. What happened after that is one of Hollywood's most enduring mysteries. What is known is that Marilyn was found dead in her Brentwood, California home by her psychiatrist on August 5, 1962, shortly after Robert Kennedy's visit. The cause of death was ruled "probable suicide by barbiturate overdose," but speculation among Hollywood insiders was that the Kennedy brothers used their mob connections to silence Marilyn forever. Once again, the Kennedy family may have acted as if the law didn't apply to them.

For Jackie Kennedy, Marilyn Monroe was the last straw. She had known about her husband's endless string of one-night stands for many years yet chose to be the good wife and turn a blind eye to the affairs. On one occasion, Jackie was showing guests around the White House when she came to the desks of John Kennedy's personal secretaries. Jackie sarcastically remarked, "These are my husband's secretaries whom he is having sex with." It was no secret that Kennedy liked to swim naked with his buxom assistants, whom the secret service nicknamed "Fiddle" and "Faddle," in the White House swimming pool while Jackie was upstairs with the children. But the public nature of this final tryst, with a nationally televised Marilyn Monroe breathlessly singing "Happy Birthday" to celebrate Kennedy's forty-fifth birthday at Madison Square Garden, was too much to take. Jackie would immediately file for divorce, which she knew would derail Kennedy's hope for reelection. JFK was persuasive, however, and he convinced Jackie to stay with him for the good of their children, the nation and his political career. He swore to Jackie that his days of messing around with Marilyn Monroe were done. He did, however, conveniently forget to mention that his affairs with Judith Exner (girlfriend of mobster Sam Giaconda), actress Angie Dickinson and a Washington, D.C. socialite named Mary Pinchot Meyer, as well as numerous other women, would continue. Mary Meyer and John F. Kennedy reportedly had about thirty trysts, and at least one source has claimed she brought marijuana or LSD to almost all of those illicit meetings. She even confided to close friends that they smoked pot together in the White House. Meyer would be mysteriously murdered in 1964.

So Jackie would continue to raise her children, Carolyn and John Jr., and the president would continue to masquerade as a wholesome family man. The first family were frequent guests to Newport throughout John's presidency, often visiting Jackie's mom, Janet, and stepfather, Hugh, at their seaside manor, Hammersmith Farm. Some of the most famous publicity photos of the young family were taken there as well, with the presidential helicopter landing on the back lawn of the estate, and the young children running out to greet their proud father.

One of the other secrets the president was able to keep throughout his term was a debilitating back injury. The president was in almost constant pain from his troublesome spine, which had plagued him since childhood and was exacerbated by the sinking of his PT boat during World War II. Fortunately for the injury-plagued Kennedy, he would cross paths with Dr. Max Jacobsen, a physician who had fled Germany before the outbreak of World War II and set up an office on the Upper West Side of Manhattan. Dubbed "Dr. Feelgood," Jacobson was known for his "miracle tissue regenerator" shots, which consisted of amphetamines,

The presidential helicopter touches down at Hammersmith Farm in Newport for a visit with the in-laws, Hugh and Janet Auchincloss. President Kennedy was a frequent visitor here during his presidency, earning the estate the nickname the "Summer White House." *Photo courtesy of the White House Archives.*

vitamins, painkillers and human placenta. Dr. Jacobsen first administered these miracle shots to JFK just before his decisive televised debates against Richard Nixon in 1960, the same debates that swayed votes in Kennedy's favor. Kennedy was also receiving shots of cortisone to relieve his back pain, and one of the side effects of this painkiller is an orange glow to the skin. His healthy glow, which made him more look appealing to voters during the televised debates, was actually a byproduct of his repeated use of cortisone to mask his ailing back. This is just one more example of the Kennedy family myth and how they would always seem to hide or manipulate the truth from the unsuspecting public.

By 1962, Jackie Kennedy was spending much more time away from Washington, D.C., and an increasing amount of time with her mother, Janet, in Newport. There was even speculation that she was leaving the president and moving full time to Hammersmith Farm, although these rumors never came to fruition. The president had made a concerted effort to spend time with his wife and young children and was a regular visitor to Newport in 1962. He would frequently be seen walking the beach with his young son and enjoying the America's Cup yacht races in and around Newport Harbor. Kennedy felt at ease on the water and always seemed to be relaxed while spending time in the City by the Sea. Kennedy also had close democratic allies in Newport, including longtime Senate companion Claiborne Pell. Perhaps Kennedy was trying to reconnect with his family, repair his personal and private image and put the Marilyn Monroe affair behind him for good.

Just because John Kennedy was in Newport, mending fences with his family, doesn't mean he was totally behaving himself. While Kennedy was in Newport, he liked to use the heated saltwater swimming pool at a mansion called Fairholme, which was owned by Robert and Anita O'Keefe Young. Mr. Young was a successful investment banker who knew JFK from Palm Beach, and Mrs. Young was a staunch supporter of the president and the Democratic Party. She was also the sister of noted American

President Kennedy is seen here enjoying a day on the water, watching the 1962 America's Cup yacht races just off the Newport coast. The young man in the foreground is John Kerry, former senator from Massachusetts. It is tragic when you realize that a little over a year from the date this picture was taken, the president would be felled by an assassin's bullet in Dallas, Texas. *Photo courtesy of the White House Archives.*

landscape artist Georgia O'Keefe, who was also a frequent guest at the mansion. On Kennedy's many trips to Newport, the Fairholme pool was his salvation as the spot to rehab his chronic bad back. Kennedy was an early riser, and while in Newport, he always began his swims at 8:00 a.m. with a contingent of Secret Service men guarding the pool and the nearby rooftops. But the staff at the mansion noticed something peculiar while the president was in town: he would arrive early in the morning, before sunrise, unescorted by Secret Service; pick up a female Fairholme house guest; and disappear with her for a couple of hours. The president would return to drop off his companion a short time later and then, with his entourage of bodyguards, begin his 8:00 a.m. swim. How Kennedy was able to elude his family and his security, drive his car a few miles to rendezvous with his early morning companion and return with her unnoticed was a mystery, but it does demonstrate the lengths to which the former president would go for a little extramarital action. Kennedy was even planning on renting the adjacent estate to Hammersmith Farm, a property called Armsea, for the upcoming 1964 summer season in Newport, reportedly to stash his mistresses. However, those plans would be altered after a trip to Dallas in November 1963.

On November 22, 1963, President Kennedy was assassinated in Dallas, Texas, while riding in a limousine with his wife, Texas governor John Connally and Connally's wife, Nellie. The suspected assassin, Lee Harvey Oswald, was arrested and subsequently murdered two days later by Dallas nightclub owner and mafia acquaintance Jack Ruby. With Oswald's murder, questions would linger for decades about whom JFK's true assassin really was. Was it a pro–Fidel Castro faction that wanted revenge for Kennedy's attempts to oust the Cuban dictator? Was it Vice President Lyndon Johnson, who, with Kennedy out of the way, would become president? Or was it the mafia, which had helped elect Kennedy, who then turned his back on his powerful allies while Attorney General Robert Kennedy stepped up prosecution of the organized crime families? One thing is for sure: John Kennedy had made many powerful enemies, and someone exacted his revenge with an assassin's bullet that day in Dallas. With his assassination, it also closed the chapter on his so-called storybook presidency, nicknamed "Camelot."

JFK's mystique was largely a creation of his well-connected father, his outstanding charisma mixed with charm and the assistance of some powerful yet sinister allies. It is ironic that these same ingredients that made him so popular, along with his own sense of invincibility, were also

One of the most iconic photos of the president and his son was taken at Newport's exclusive Bailey's Beach. The president was a frequent visitor to Newport in 1962, reconnecting with his family and enjoying the America's Cup yacht races. After President Kennedy's assassination in 1963, Newport would lose a little bit of its luster and would never truly be the same with the end of "Camelot." *Photo courtesy of Robert Knudson, National Archives.*

the same forces that led to his downfall. When the assassin's bullet struck down and killed President Kennedy, a little of the charm and aura of Newport died along with him, and Newport would never feel quite as it had before his untimely demise.

# CHAPTER 15

# THE UNPLUGGED CONTROVERSY

Even to this day, there are still a lot of unanswered questions about the events that took place onstage the evening of Sunday, July 25, 1965. The headliner for the Newport Folk Festival, one of the preeminent music festivals in the country, had just taken the stage and was about to begin the final set of the wildly successful show. The hillside location, just north of the downtown area, called Festival Field, was crowded with an estimated eight thousand people, who by early evening were anxiously anticipating the festival's star performer.

Peter Yarrow, from the band Peter, Paul and Mary and master of ceremonies, finally called the event's star onstage: "Ladies and gentlemen, the person that's going to come up now has a limited amount of time…His name is Bob Dylan."

And with that introduction, folk music legend Bob Dylan began his first song, called "Maggie's Farm," playing electric guitar along with the members of a band known as the Paul Butterfield Blues Band. Playing electric guitar was a departure for Dylan, who was better known for his acoustic guitar as well as the harmonica. Dylan was also unfamiliar with his backup band, which had rehearsed only three songs with him the night before the fateful concert.

During the first song, a smattering of boos and cheers could be heard among the crowd. Dylan and his band moved into their second song, a rendition of his soon-to-be hit "Like a Rolling Stone," and then into a third song called "Phantom Engineer." After playing "Phantom Engineer," Dylan told the band, "Let's go, man. That's all." and walked off stage. The sound of loud booing and clapping could be heard in the background. Peter Yarrow returned to the microphone and begged Dylan to continue performing. Apparently desperate to appease the audience, he assured them that Dylan was "just getting his axe" even before it was clear whether he would be willing to return solo. Dylan was, by some accounts, highly distressed. Eventually coaxed back onstage by Yarrow and Joan Baez, he realized he didn't have the right harmonica and lashed out at Yarrow: "What are you doing to me?" he protested.

Yarrow's public pleading for Dylan to return to the stage was clearly a spur-of-the-moment ploy to soothe the crowd. The band couldn't return because it had only rehearsed three songs, so Dylan was essentially being forced to perform an impromptu acoustic set on a night when plugging in was a major artistic statement. And Dylan, his voice betraying real nervousness and distress, had to beg the audience for "an E harmonica." Within a few moments, a clatter of harmonicas hit the stage. He then sang two songs to the now-silent audience, "It's All Over Now, Baby Blue" and "Mr. Tambourine Man." The crowd exploded with applause at the end, calling for more and chanting, "We want Bob! We want Bob!"

After the controversial concert, the rumors ran rampant, and the myth of the folk festival began: Bob Dylan was booed off the stage because he

Bob Dylan was one of the most popular musicians and outspoken political activists of the 1960s. Seen here with Joan Baez, another frequent performer at the Newport Folk Festival, Dylan was widely criticized when he left his traditional folk music roots and played an electric guitar at the 1965 Newport Folk Festival. *Photo courtesy of Wikimedia commons.*

played an electric guitar and turned his back on his folk music roots. Where the legend began is unknown, and many people who were in attendance would vehemently dispute this claim. It's true there were boos in the crowd, but it may not have been Dylan's choice of instrument that caused the ruckus. One possible explanation for the booing was that audience members were upset by poor sound quality and the surprisingly short set. The sound quality was certainly the reason Pete Seeger, legendary folk musician and festival co-founder, disliked the performance. He said he went to the sound system and told the technicians, "Get that distortion out of his voice... It's terrible. If I had an axe, I'd chop the microphone cable right now." Seeger also said, however, that he only wanted to cut the cables because he wanted the audience to hear Dylan's lyrics properly; he thought they were important. Rumors that Seeger actually had an axe, or that a festival board member wanted to pull out the entire electrical wiring system, were

Bob Dylan is seen here with his trademark acoustic guitar and harmonica. It is still not known to this day whether people in the crowd were booing because Dylan was playing an electric guitar or because they were angered by the show's poor production quality. *Photo courtesy of Wikimedia commons.*

never substantiated. The tapes of the concerts have even been analyzed by sound engineers, and the findings show that the booing was directed at Peter Yarrow. Yarrow upset the crowd when he attempted to keep Dylan's spot to its proper length rather than let the crowd hear more of his music. There's nothing to indicate the crowd disliked Dylan's music, electrified or not.

At Bob Dylan's next few concerts, the crowds were noticeably more hostile to the folk/rock star. He would play half of his concerts in his old acoustic style and then the rest of the show with electric guitars. Many concertgoers were upset at Dylan for what they perceived as him turning his back on his folk music roots. At one concert where a crowd member called Dylan "Judas," the lead signer instructed the band to play louder and drown out the disgruntled audience member. There was no doubt that Dylan's relationship with his fans would be contemptuous over the next few years, but he would persevere and become one of the most beloved and prolific musicians. Dylan had also made a promise to himself never to return to the Newport Folk Festival after the controversy that took place in 1965. That stance would eventually soften over time when Bob Dylan played to record crowds at the 2002 festival held at Fort Adams State Park overlooking Newport Harbor. Dylan was received warmly and surprised the crowd when he appeared onstage wearing a wig and a fake beard. Perhaps he was trying to poke fun at his last Newport appearance thirty-seven years earlier, or maybe he was hiding his identity from those still angry at his previous performance when he plugged in and went electric, forever changing his musical personality.

## CHAPTER 16

# A FALLEN STAR

Betty Hutton was one of Hollywood's fastest-rising starlets in the 1940s and '50s, and in the blink of an eye, her career was over. Hutton, born Betty June Thornburg in Battle Creek, Michigan, in 1921, started entertaining at the age of three in her family's speakeasy after her father abandoned her mother for another woman. Hutton sang and danced in the saloon, along with her sister, to support their now fatherless family. She got her big break in 1942, appearing in a film called *The Fleet's In* with Paramount Pictures' number one female star, Dorothy Lamour. With the 1945 release of *Incendiary Blonde*, Betty Hutton had supplanted Lamour as Paramount's number one female box office attraction.

Now dubbed the original "Blond Bombshell," the wildly popular Betty Hutton went on to make nineteen feature films between 1942 and 1952. She was so popular during World War II that she was frequently chosen to entertain the troops on USO tours throughout Europe to boost the soldiers' morale. Hutton was also considered a top-rate dancer, even receiving the top billing over Fred Astaire in the 1950 musical *Let's Dance*. Hutton's greatest screen triumph came in *Annie Get Your Gun* for MGM, which hired her to replace an irrational and problematic Judy Garland in the role of Annie Oakley. The film—and the leading role, which was retooled for Hutton—was a smash hit, with the biggest critical praise going to Hutton. Her performance was described as "a brassy, energetic performance with a voice that could sound like a fire alarm." Hutton, however, like Garland, was earning a reputation for being extremely difficult to work with. She was headed down a thorny path, one that led to alcoholism and an addiction to prescription drugs, especially sleeping pills.

Betty Hutton's silver-screen zenith came in 1952, when she was chosen to star in famed director Cecil B. Deville's big-budget production *The Greatest Show on Earth*, which showed life inside the Ringling Bros. and Barnum & Bailey Circus. Hutton played a trapeze artist in one of the highest-grossing films of all time, alongside immortal Hollywood luminaries Charlton Heston and Jimmy Stewart. The film even won the 1952 academy award for best picture, and Betty Hutton was the most famous actress in the world. Just like that, her career was, for all intents and purposes, over. Hutton made a strategic career move that backfired horribly when she insisted her then husband, Charles O'Curran, direct her next film. When Paramount Studios declined, Hutton tore up her contract and essentially committed occupational suicide. She had also severely injured her arm in the filming of *The Greatest Show on Earth*, and this only intensified her use of painkillers and alcohol.

The rest of the 1950s and '60s would prove to be difficult for the former Queen of the Silver Screen. She would try her hand at television, but her shows were total flops and would eventually be cancelled. Bit roles and low-budget films were about the only jobs that came her way. By 1970, Hutton had lost her singing voice, her mother had died in a house fire and she nearly died from a sleeping pill overdose. Betty Hutton would hit rock bottom in 1972 while performing at a Framingham, Massachusetts dinner theater when she discovered she had lost custody of her daughter Carolyn, whom she had during her fourth and final marriage. Hutton had lost her will to live, and the pills were no longer able to level her out. She was checked into a nearby drug rehabilitation facility weighing only eighty-five pounds and looking more dead than alive. It was inside this facility that Betty Hutton would meet the man she said would save her life.

That man was Father Peter Maguire, pastor of Saint Anthony's Church in Portsmouth, Rhode Island. Father Maguire was at the rehab center to check on the status of his cook, and while there, he befriended Betty Hutton. Father Maguire would invite the former starlet to continue her rehab at the church rectory, a place she would remain for the next five years of her life. The one-time Hollywood idol was now cooking, making beds and cleaning rooms with a vigor she hadn't felt since her early days on the silver screen. When her recovery was complete, she settled into a bona fide Newport mansion overlooking the harbor and enrolled in classes at nearby Salve Regina University. In 1986, the once down-and-out former performer

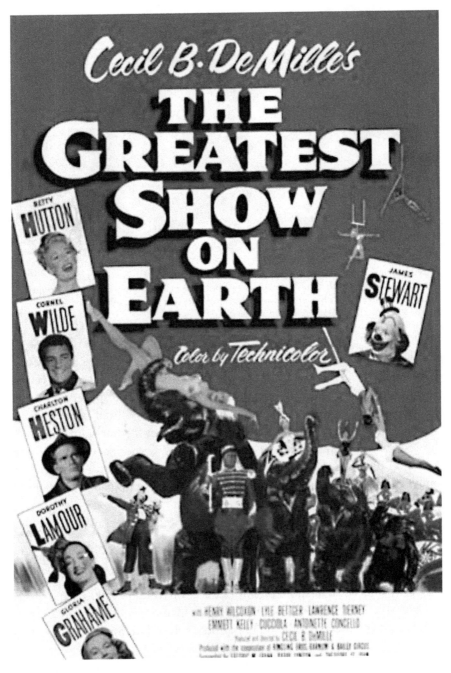

Once the biggest female star in Hollywood, Betty Hutton eventually wound up working at a Newport-area soup kitchen because of drug and alcohol abuse. This movie poster from *The Greatest Show on Earth* shows Betty Hutton with top billing over silver screen legends Charlton Heston and Jimmy Stewart. *Photo courtesy of Wikimedia commons.*

Betty Hutton literally rubbed elbows with the biggest names in Hollywood. Here Betty is seen cheek-to-cheek with show business legend Bob Hope. The comedy duo was a frequent visitor to military bases all over the world during World War II in an effort to boost the troops' morale. *Photo courtesy of Wikimedia commons.*

graduated cum laude with a master's degree in liberal studies and would go on to share her passion for acting as a professor of drama at Salve Regina University and Emerson College in nearby Boston. Betty Hutton was reborn, like a phoenix rising from the ashes. Without a doubt, she credited Father Maguire and her time in Newport for her salvation, and she rediscovered an inner peace she had rarely experienced before her addiction to drugs and alcohol. Now clean and sober, Betty Hutton was enjoying her later years giving back to a community that she credited for part of her liberation from substance abuse.

Father Maguire would pass away in 1996, and Betty couldn't bear the thought of living in Newport without her spiritual advisor. She would move to Palm Springs, California, to be near family and friends who would be there to lend support in her constant battle to stay sober. Betty Hutton would pass away from complications of colon cancer on March 11, 2007, at the age of eighty-six. Betty Hutton was gone, but her memory would live on forever, with her image frozen in time on numerous reels of film and her star on the Hollywood walk of fame. But more importantly, her story of perseverance against the perils of drug and alcohol abuse, her can-do spirit and the lives she touched with the help of her mentor, Father Maguire, will forever be the former "Blond Bombshell's" most meaningful and enduring contribution to the world she left behind.

# CHAPTER 17

# BOY BAND GONE BAD

Don't feel bad if you aren't familiar with Newport's version of the Backstreet Boys, 'N Sync or the Jackson 5. It's true that there was a can't-miss family band from Newport once destined for stardom, vowing to become the American version of the Beatles. This teen quartet got its start playing Newport-area hotel lounges and waterfront bars on Bannister's Wharf. The group became so popular that it appeared on *The Tonight Show*, *The Today Show* and *The Ed Sullivan Show*, twice. It even inspired the hit TV series *The Partridge Family* and was originally offered the show itself but turned it down when actress and singer Shirley Jones was chosen as the band's mom. The group, which was managed by the members' father, missed out on a golden opportunity to accelerate its meteoric rise to stardom by passing on the sitcom. This mistake, coupled with financial mismanagement and family squabbling, ended the pop group's ascent to fame almost as fast as it began. That band was the Cowsills.

The Cowsills moved to Newport from Canton, Ohio, in the mid-1950s when Bud Cowsill, a navy recruiter, was reassigned with his growing and musically inclined clan. His sons specialized in great harmonies and the ability to sing and play music at an early age; they even performed for their church congregation and on Cleveland-area TV stations before the age of ten. The band was officially formed in 1965, when brothers Billy, Bob and Barry started performing at Newport-area venues and school dances. When brother John joined the band as a drummer in 1967, Barry switched to bass guitar, and Newport's Fab Four was off and running. The Cowsills were renowned for their ability to accurately replicate Beatles tunes and mimicked their idols in clubs and hotel ballrooms for up to four hours at a time. By 1967, three other members were added to the family act, including mom Barbara, and the Cowsills would sign a recording contract with MGM records. They would record one of their most popular singles, "The Rain, the Park and Other Things," which would make the young group teen idols worldwide. "The Rain, the Park and Other Things" wound up reaching number two on the Billboard charts, selling some three million copies in its first release. This bubbly, effervescent and cheerful tune is easily recognizable, and you have probably heard it at least a dozen times, although you probably weren't really sure who performed it. The Cowsills were also paid spokespeople for the American Dairy Association, becoming the first band to appear in advertisements promoting milk. By 1968, the busy group was on the road, doing up to two hundred live performances on the concert circuit, and it recorded another top two hit with the theme song for the popular musical *Hair*. But just about the time they reached their musical zenith, things started to unravel, and a series of events would doom the Cowsills' march to music immortality.

The first major bombshell occurred in 1969 when lead singer and most popular member, Billy, was thrown out of the band by his father and manager, Bud, for smoking marijuana. The Cowsills would continue their prolific schedule for the next couple years, but the band just wasn't the same. Mom Barbara even landed in the hospital to recuperate from exhaustion. Perhaps the band had lost its magic touch or the public grew tired of "bubble gum pop." By 1972, the group had basically disbanded, with the individual members striking out on their own. In 1975, Bud Cowsill filed for bankruptcy, listing debts of over $450,000 owed to hotels, airlines and credit card companies. His assets were listed at less than $5,000.

Over the next three decades, the Cowsills would occasionally reunite to play various festivals and state fairs, but most of the members continued music careers on their own. Oldest member Billy moved to western Canada and found a niche playing country music. John Cowsill found success as a member of the Beach Boys touring band, playing drums and keyboard and singing background vocals. Arguably, the most successful and prolific former member of the Cowsills was youngest member Susan. She joined a band called the Continental Drifters and eventually formed her own successful group, the Susan Cowsill Band, which still performs numerous concerts annually. In 2000, the seven surviving Cowsill members performed at the waterfront festival, A Taste of Rhode Island, only two blocks from the Newport Wharf where the young band originally got its start some thirty-five years earlier. Sadly, the group's dynamo, diminutive mom Barbara, had passed away in 1985, and dad Bud, who had mismanaged the band's proceeds, died in 1992.

In 2005, tragedy would again strike the Cowsills. Both Barry and Susan were living in New Orleans when Hurricane Katrina pummeled the Crescent City. Fortunately, Susan and her husband had fled before the massive hurricane flooded the city, but Barry remained behind, vowing to see his sister soon. Despite numerous attempts to contact her brother, Susan was never able to track him down. On December 28, 2005, a badly decomposed body was found floating under a city pier. There was a handwritten note found in the pants pocket, with the name, address and

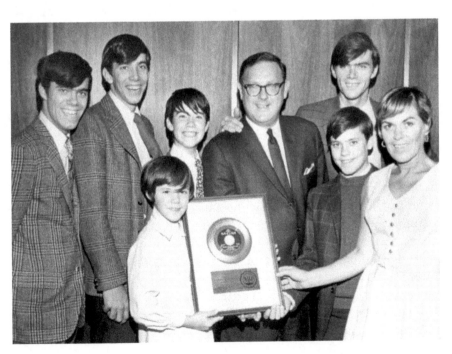

The Cowsills were a musical act from Newport that was extremely popular during the late 1960s and spawned the musical genre "bubble gum pop." Here the family is seen collecting their gold record for the song "The Rain, the Park and Other Things." *Photo courtesy of Wikimedia commons.*

If you were a fan of the TV show *The Partridge Family*, you can thank the Newport band the Cowsills. The Cowsills were the inspiration for the 1970s program about a traveling musical family living out of a colorful bus. *Photo courtesy of Wikimedia commons.*

phone number of the unidentifiable corpse, Barry Cowsill. A memorial service was scheduled for February 18, 2006, to honor the life of the fallen band and family member when heartbreaking news arrived from western Canada. Oldest brother Billy had perished the evening before his brother's memorial service from various ailments, culminating from a lifetime of drug and alcohol abuse. Family and friends learned of Billy's passing at Barry's memorial service, held at King Park overlooking the harbor, the site of one of the Cowsills' first public concerts. The location is just down the hill from the family's Newport home, Halidon Hall, and Barry's ashes were spread over the area where he and his siblings had performed more than forty years earlier. There is also a bench in King Park dedicated to the pair of musical brothers, so anyone who visits the harbor-side common can see where it all started for Newport's version of the Partridge Family.

No one can say for sure how the Cowsills' future might have been different had they accepted the offer to be TV's original family band, roving the country in a brightly painted bus. Would the popularity of the show have catapulted them to TV immortality? Or were the Cowsills victims of their era, destined to be popular for only a short time, briefly capitalizing on the nation's brief love affair with "bubble gum pop"? The latter is probably a more likely outcome, but one thing is certain: Newport's boy band could have become TV's first modern-day "reality show."

# CHAPTER 18

# THE SCULPTOR'S DOWNFALL

One of the most impressive mansions in Newport, Rhode Island, is a property called Beacon Rock. It sits prominently on a rock outcropping almost hovering over the harbor, with unparalleled views of the entire waterfront and the Newport Bridge. The "Acropolis of Newport," as it is commonly called, was completed in 1891 for Newport Yacht Club commodore Edwin Morgan, a distant cousin of renowned financier J.P. Morgan. Stanford White was the architect commissioned to design this impressive property and completed it in just over three years. White was a prolific architect, designing some of Newport's most famous structures, including the Tennis Hall of Fame building and Rosecliff mansion, as well as the original Madison Square Garden in New York City. But construction of the mansion wasn't easy. The location on the rocky hillside had to be dynamited repeatedly to make the top of the promontory flat enough for construction to begin. But Edwin Morgan didn't care about the price; he wanted his replica Greek palace to be one of the finest ever designed in Newport, and he got his wish. Edwin Morgan would go on to be one of the most decorated yachtsmen in the world with his defense of the prestigious America's Cup trophy. Commodore Morgan presided over the Newport Yacht club for three decades and even kept some of the America's Cup defending yachts anchored in the bay just below the impressive columned mansion.

In 1951, world-famous sculptor Felix de Weldon purchased the home for the unbelievably low price of $100,000. De Weldon's name might not be familiar to you, but most people will recognize his most famous work, the United States Marine Corps War Memorial, just outside the main

Beacon Rock sits magnificently on a rocky cliff top and offers unparalleled views of the harbor, the Rose Island Lighthouse and the Newport Bridge. Built in 1891, the "Acropolis of Newport," as it is called, was once owned by renowned sculptor Felix de Weldon. De Weldon was forced to sell his beloved property to repay bank loans incurred while caring for his ailing wife. *Photo courtesy of the author.*

gate of Arlington National Cemetery in Virginia. Most people know it as the Iwo Jima statue. This seventy-eight-foot-high, one-hundred-ton bronze work captures the exact moment the American flag was being raised on Mount Suribachi during the brutal battle over the tiny island in the South Pacific near the end of World War II. This work catapulted Felix de Weldon to international fame. He created more than two thousand monuments spread over seven continents, including a statue of Admiral Byrd in Antarctica, during his prolific career and was known as the sculptor to presidents and kings. His bronze bust of assassinated president John F. Kennedy was so lifelike that it reportedly brought Jacqueline Kennedy to tears after witnessing it for the first time at its unveiling at the JFK Presidential Library just outside Boston.

Unfortunately for Felix de Weldon, he was a much better sculptor than he was a financier. His financial troubles started when his wife developed Alzheimer's in the mid-1980s, and de Weldon was forced to take out loans to cover her treatment expenses. He used his eleven-acre waterfront Newport mansion, Beacon Rock, as collateral to cover the $500-per-day medical bills. The Bank of New England, which lent de Weldon the money, threatened to foreclose, but the Austrian-born sculptor kept assuring the bank that the loans would be repaid. The final straw was when the Bank of New England failed in 1991 and was seized by the Federal Deposit Insurance Corporation. The FDIC quickly went after the largest outstanding loan on the former Bank of New England's books: Beacon Rock. It turns out that with the loan interest and penalties, the sculptor's debt was in excess of $3.8 million and mounting daily. The FDIC forced Felix de Weldon into involuntary bankruptcy, and the house would be auctioned to pay the mounting debts. Apparently, de

Weldon was irate about how the FDIC handled his case, claiming that this treatment would never occur in other nations: "In most countries like France or Italy, a great artist is a national hero and they do everything for him. In this country they just try to take everything away from me and ruin me."

De Weldon did everything in his power to thwart the sale of his beloved waterfront mansion, including locking the doors so perspective buyers couldn't view the home before the auction was held. On auction day, only $1 million was offered for the property, well below the $3 million minimum price the FDIC required for the sale, so de Weldon continued to live on the premises for at least a little while longer, until another property liquidation auction could be scheduled. To complicate matters even further, police were called to the property by a neighbor, only to discover de Weldon's son Byron had broken into the house and was stealing valuable antiques. He claimed he was removing them to protect his father's valuable assets, but the police didn't buy it. The younger de Weldon was ordered to enter a drug rehabilitation center as part of his sentencing. The legal wrangling would drag on until 1996, when the home was finally sold to a prominent local attorney, who painstakingly restored Beacon Rock to its original grandeur.

With his wife gone, his beloved mansion gone and his son in and out of trouble with the law, things seemed bleak for Felix de Weldon. Close friends of de Weldon commented after this ordeal that he seemed at peace, almost jovial— perhaps relieved that the entire ordeal was finally behind him. He retreated

The raising of the flag on Iwo Jima is sculptor Felix de Weldon's most famous work. This massive bronze statue stands at the gate of Arlington National Cemetery in Virginia and honors the men and women of the U.S. Marines who lost their lives defending our country. *Photo courtesy of the author.*

to his Virginia farm, where he would continue to work on his sculpting until his last days, passing away in 2003 at the age of ninety-six.

With Felix de Weldon's passing, America had lost its most famous and prolific sculptor. His works still awe and inspire millions of people every year, and his legacy will live on for generations. It is a bit sad, however, to think such a gifted man who devoted years of his life sculpting some of the most historic events and heroic figures of our nation couldn't be given some latitude. Especially given the circumstances from which the financial hardship arose, it's difficult to image some concessions could not be reached. Unfortunately, no deal could be struck, and Felix de Weldon would lose Beacon Rock. However, de Weldon should not be remembered for his financial woes but rather for the indelible creations and artwork he left behind and for what he did best: sculpt.

# CHAPTER 19

# ONE, TWO, THREE, JUMP

August 31, 1990, was one of those wonderful late summer evenings in Rhode Island. Adam and Elena Emery were doing what generations of Rhode Islanders had done before them—enjoying an evening out in Warwick at the iconic Rocky Point Amusement Park.

Rocky Point was the place where countless people wistfully spent their summers enjoying the wide variety of rides, food and amusements the theme park offered. The park opened in the late 1840s, operating until 1995, and was known for its rides like the log flume, Ferris wheel and corkscrew-loop roller coaster. If you ask most people about their favorite memories of the amusement park, many will hearken back to the Shore Dinner Hall, famous for its clam cakes, steamers and New England clam chowder. This massive dining room on the banks of Narragansett Bay could seat a whopping four thousand people at one time.

The recently married couple sat blissfully in their car, enjoying their clam cakes and chowder, without a care in the world, when suddenly an incident occurred that would change their lives forever. Out of nowhere, a car sideswiped their 1985 Ford Thunderbird, smashing the taillight and then speeding away. Elena Emery was outraged, screaming at her husband to "Go get them!" and pointing at a 1975 red Ford LTD leaving the parking lot. Adam Emery quickly complied to his screaming wife's request and was soon in high-speed pursuit of the alleged hit-and-run culprit. The Emerys chased the car they thought had dented them for more than two miles, honking the horn repeatedly and flashing the headlights in an attempt to stop the red

Ford LTD. Finally, Emery pulled in front of the runaway driver, forcing him to stop, and Elena Emory quickly handed her husband a two-sided survival knife, just in case. The two men inside the red LTD were terrified. Twenty-year-old Jason Bass, a Rocky Point concession worker, and his seventeen-year-old cousin Joshua Post were being confronted by a knife-wielding man screaming, "I'm going to kill you!" The two frightened young men thought Adam Emory must be drunk. Why else would he be screaming murderous threats at them? They had no idea what was going on, and for good reason. As confirmed by paint chip analysis later on, Elena Emory had pointed out the wrong car. These two young men were just heading home after Jason Bass's shift, unaware that someone had damaged the Emorys' vehicle.

But Adam Emory saw blood and wanted revenge for his broken taillight, ignoring the young man's plea of innocence. Adam Emory didn't listen. Emery leaned inside the driver's side window just as Jason Bass threw the car in reverse. As Emery hung on to the side of the vehicle, he plunged the knife into Bass's chest in an attempt to stop the now out-of-control car. The LTD finally crashed into a guardrail, but it was too late. Twenty-year-old Jason Bass was dead, his heart punctured by the knife. Adam Emery was arrested and charged with murder—all over a dented bumper and broken taillight.

On November 11, 1993, Adam Emory was convicted of second-degree murder, despite his plea of self-defense and trying to blame his wife for egging him on. He seemed rather stoic and unemotional when the verdict was read, mouthing something to his wife. A lip-reading expert hired to review the courtroom video to determine what he said came to this conclusion: Adam Emery told his wife, "We will do what we originally said; we should have done this earlier. You promised me." Emery was freed on a $270,000 bond awaiting sentencing, which could have been up to twenty years in prison. But Adam Emery had no desire to spend twenty years in prison; he had other ideas. When Adam and Elena Emory left the courtroom that day, it would be the last time they were ever seen alive.

At 6:50 p.m. that same day, a Rhode Island state trooper pulled up behind an abandoned Toyota Camry at the peak of the Newport Bridge. The car was still running, with the key in the ignition, parking lights on and nobody inside. The officer also found the packaging for eighty pounds of exercise weights, cut-up credit cards and the driver's licenses belonging to a local couple, Adam and Elena Emory. A team of police divers, dredgers and sonar-equipped rescue boats searched the area almost two hundred feet below the bridge's roadbed for any sign of the couple, but not a trace was found. According to Newport police captain Robert McQueeny, all the evidence pointed to a mutual suicide. The Emerys wanted to make it look like they had stopped the car at the top of the bridge, donned the body weights and plummeted off the bridge to their deaths. But no witnesses on the bridge saw anyone jump, and no trace of the couple's bodies were found in the turbulent waters below.

If someone were planning a suicide, the Newport Pell Bridge would be an ideal location. Completed in 1969 at a cost of over $50 million, the highest point of the span is over two hundred feet above Narragansett Bay. In 1992, the bridge was named after longtime Democratic Rhode Island senator Claiborne Pell, and the overpass has seen dozens of people jump to their deaths from its heights since its completion. It is highly unlikely that anyone could survive the leap. But Newport police captain Robert McQueeny wasn't convinced that the Emerys had actually jumped. He speculated that since no one had seen them go over the side and no trace of their bodies was found below, the Emerys had staged their suicide, jumped into a waiting car and were on the run, perhaps attempting to leave the country.

However, about a year after the Emerys' disappearance, a discovery was made that would shoot huge holes in Captain McQueeny's theory that the suicide was faked. Elena Emery's skull was pulled from the bay in the net of a local fisherman near the east piling of the Newport Bridge. A subsequent search of the area turned up leg bones, confirmed to be Elena's with a DNA check. Elena Emery was dead, but Adam seemed to have vanished into thin air. Was he dead also, having jumped to his death with his wife? Or was he still alive, sacrificing his wife to hatch his elaborate escape plan? A new theory had evolved that showed the desperation of a guilty man and how he would do anything to keep his freedom. Was it possible that Adam and Elena had really planned to commit suicide together, leaving this life hand-in-hand as they fell to their deaths? Or was it possible that Adam had convinced Elena that this was the plan all along until the pair was actually standing at the rail preparing to jump. Did Adam say goodbye to his wife, telling her that on the count of three they would go over the side, and then count, "One, two, three, jump!" Except at the word jump, Adam Emery released her hand, watched her fall two hundred feet to her death, jumped into the car of an accomplice and was whisked away from the scene in an attempt to flee the country. The evidence suggests that this might have been the case. Close friends of Adam claim that before the trial, he had taken up studying Italian, perhaps in an attempt to set up a new identity in Europe. Although he was declared legally dead in 2004, the FBI placed Adam Emery on its most wanted list in 2010, lending some credence to the possibility that the

# WANTED
## BY THE FBI

**Unlawful Flight to Avoid Prosecution - Second Degree Murder**

## ADAM C. EMERY

### DESCRIPTION

| | | | |
|---|---|---|---|
| **Date(s) of Birth Used:** | November 10, 1962 | **Hair:** | Brown |
| **Place of Birth:** | Rhode Island | **Eyes:** | Blue |
| **Height:** | 6'1" | **Sex:** | Male |
| **Weight:** | 175 pounds | **Race:** | White |
| **NCIC:** | W785425698 | **Nationality:** | American |
| **Occupations:** | Purchasing Agent, Worker in a Plastics Company | | |
| **Scars and Marks:** | None known | | |
| **Remarks:** | Emery may travel to Florida or Italy. | | |

### CAUTION

Adam C. Emery was convicted of second degree murder in Rhode Island State Superior Court on November 10, 1993. The conviction stemmed from an incident which occurred in August of 1990 during which Emery stabbed another man to death. Emery was permitted to remain free on bail pending formal sentencing which was scheduled for December of 1993. He left the courthouse in order to get his affairs in order. Hours after his release, his car was located on the top of the Newport Bridge in Newport, Rhode Island. Emery has not been seen since the time of his release. A federal warrant was issued on January 18, 1994, and Emery was charged with unlawful flight to avoid prosecution.

SHOULD BE CONSIDERED ARMED AND DANGEROUS

If you have any information concerning this person, please contact your local FBI office or the nearest American Embassy or Consulate.

This was the original FBI wanted poster for fugitive murderer Adam Emery. Emery was convicted of murder in 1993 for stabbing a man after a fender-bender at a local amusement park. Emery walked out of the courtroom on bail, never to be seen again, disappearing without a trace. *Photo courtesy of the FBI's most wanted.*

suicide was just an attempt to throw authorities off his trail long enough to escape. It appears, considering the evidence, that it might have worked.

It is amazing to think the events that transpired on August 31, 1990, would have such a bizarre and unbelievable outcome. What started out as a fun night out at a local amusement park turned into the murder of an innocent young man, the suicide of a devoted wife and the disappearance of another man—all over a fender-bender and a broken taillight. We will never really know what was going through the mind of Adam Emery that late

The last clue to Adam Emery's whereabouts was found atop the Newport Bridge a few hours after his murder conviction in 1993. His abandoned car was found parked at the very peak of the bridge, with empty packages for diving weights inside. The evidence suggested that Emery and his wife, Elena, weighed themselves down and then plunged off the two-hundred-foot-high platform to their deaths in a suicide pact. *Photo courtesy of Stephanie Izzo Photography.*

summer evening in 1990. We will never know what his motive was or why his rage over a small dent in his car would become so intense that it would cause him to take another human life. One thing is for sure, however: given the circumstances that transpired, it is unlikely Adam Emery would react the way he did if he could do it all over again. It is also likely that next time you drive over the Newport Bridge, you will pause and think about Elena Emory and her last few moments alive, just before she gave up her life for her soon-to-be-fugitive husband.

# BIBLIOGRAPHY

Blanco, Richard L., and Paul J. Sanborn. *The American Revolution: 1775–1783: An Encyclopedia*. New York: Garland, 1993.

Bugliosi, Vincent. *Four Days in November: The Assassination of President John F. Kennedy*. New York: W.W. Norton and Company, 2008.

D'Antonio, Michael. *A Full Cup: Sir Thomas Lipton's Extraordinary Life and His Quest for the America's Cup*. N.p.: Riverhead Trade, 2011.

Feifer, George. *Breaking Open Japan: Commodore Perry, Lord Abe and American Imperialism in 1853*. Washington, D.C.: Smithsonian Publishing, 2006.

Grogan, David. "Grave Doubts." People Magazine.com. 1994.

Hutton, Betty. *Backstage You Can Have My Story*. N.p.: Betty Hutton Estate, 2009.

Kelly, Brian, C. *Best Little Stories from the American Revolution*. N.p.: Source Books, 2011.

Loughery, John. *The Other Side of Silence*. N.p.: Henry Holt and Company, n.d.

Millard, Candice. *Destiny of a Republic: A Tale of Madness, Medicine and the Murder of a President*. N.p.: Anchor Publishing, 2012.

*Newport Daily News*, 1965, 1993.

*New York Times*, 1921.

Onarato, Ronald. *AIA Guide to Newport, RI*. N.p.: Avon Hill Books, 2007.

Plimpton, Ruth Talbot. *Mary Dyer: The Diary of a Rebel Quaker*. N.p.: Branden Publishing Company, 1994.

Reeves, Richard. *A Portrait of Camelot: A Thousand Days in the Kennedy White House*. N.p.: Abrams Publishing, 2010.

Scotti, R.A. *Sudden Sea: The Great Hurricane of 1938*. Boston: Back Bay Publishing, 2004.

Simpson, Richard V. *America's Cup: Trials and Triumphs*. Charleston, SC: The History Press, 2010.

Skaggs, David Curtis. *Oliver Hazard Perry: Honor, Courage, and Patriotism in the Early U.S. Navy*. N.p.: Navy Institute Press, 2006.

Sounes, Howard. *Down the Highway: The Life of Bob Dylan*. New York: Grove Press, 2011.

Spencer, Terry D'Amoto. *A Daring Feat in a Time of Need*. N.p.: Warwick Beacon, 2012.

Vanderbilt, Arthur T., II. *Fortune's Children: The Fall of the House of Vanderbilt*. New York: William Morrow, 1998.

# ABOUT THE AUTHOR

L arry Stanford, a native of Newport, Rhode Island, currently works as an information specialist at the Newport Visitors' Center. He founded Ghost Tours of Newport in 2002. He has previously published *Wicked Newport* with The History Press.

*Visit us at*
www.historypress.net

............................................................

*This title is also available as an e-book*